Da _____ ght-
ful _____ and
acc _____ rary
mo _____ this
ric _____ city
mi _____ ator
to _____

BR _____
VP _____

Ha _____ sur-
pri _____ tra-
tio _____ ing
gl _____ ight
be _____ ade
fo _____ and
in _____ ith
p _____ to
sl _____ ok
li _____ art
in _____

M _____
L _____
G _____
Sh _____

As the director of a mission sending agency, every part of our work is prayer dependent. From raising up and training new missionaries to helping them stay vibrant and effective in the field, there is no part of our work that doesn't "breath in and breathe out" prayer. In *Liturgy in the Wilderness*, Dan is helping all of us find that same rhythm—a constant return to peace and clarity that comes through the Lord's Prayer as we navigate the changing course of our lives and our culture. I, for one, am deeply thankful for Dan's insight and practical help.

BOB OSBORNE
Executive Director, Serge

Liturgy in the Wilderness offers us a fresh and engaging perspective on the Lord's Prayer. Though this widely known prayer can be uttered in less than thirty seconds, this book shows us how it can—and should—impact every single area of our lives. Marotta takes us by the hand and guides us to see that while we may never get out of the wilderness, we can always move forward in hope. This book is thoughtful, filled with wise insights and engaging stories. And best of all, Marotta doesn't merely write about this important message in his book; he lives the message, too.

J. R. BRIGGS
Author of *The Sacred Overlap* and Founding Director of Kairos Partnerships

This book is like rocket fuel for ancient wisdom. It is winsome and funny. It is deep and real. Do you lack imagination? Does your faith feel fragile? You need to read this because then you can join this amazing countercultural mission: "Congratulations. Thou hast been subverted."

J. B. SIMMONS
Novelist and author of *The Awakening of Washington's Church*

In a volatile world filled with noise, it can be tempting to search for some shiny new thing to relieve the anxiety. In this book, D. J. Marotta takes a fresh look at the Lord's Prayer and reminds us of what it is: an enduring gift for the ups and downs of our journey through the wilderness. A timely read for an age marked by anxiety.

BLAINE LAY

Executive Director, RCLI (Richmond Christian Leaders Initiative)

What a gift Dan Marotta has given those of us for whom "wilderness" feels like the rule rather than the exception of life! With the courage of a convert and the tenderness of a seasoned pastor, Dan draws a map for pilgrims of all kinds, shedding fresh light not only on the Lord's Prayer but on the subversive nature of liturgy itself. By the end of the book, I have a hunch the wilderness will feel a little less wild, and God's grace a little closer at hand.

DAVID ZAHL

Author of *Seculosity* and founder of Mockingbird Ministry

How do we navigate the wilderness of modern life? How do we reimagine our place in the world? How do we allow the gospel to subvert and subdue our disordered affections? By joining Jesus in prayer. In this warm and engaging book, Dan Marotta invites us into the Lord's Prayer, leading us as a trustworthy companion on a hope-filled journey where the kingdom comes in the midst of the wilds.

JOHN W. YATES III

Editor of the Reformation Anglicanism Essential Library

Desert comes from the Hebrew meaning "disaster" or "word." Dan gets this! The deserts we find ourselves in are, in fact, disaster. But if we truly consent, they are the exact place where we hear God's Word over our lives best. Read this book and flourish in the wilderness.

AJ SHERRILL

Author of *Being with God* and *The Enneagram for Spiritual Formation*

Unless our imaginations are unleashed as we ponder the words of Jesus, and we learn to love the ancient words of saints ripened over centuries of use, we will likely miss the deeper wisdom and greater vision God has for us in navigating the pathway of Christ. This book is remarkably fresh and stimulating.

JOHN & SUSAN YATES
Authors of *Raising Kids with Character That Lasts*

I loved reading this book! Dan's writing has given me new understanding and appreciation for the Lord's Prayer. I've been praying these words for years, and this prayer has come alive in a new way. I am so grateful to have Dan as a friend. He has a joyful enthusiasm about his work and cares deeply about everyone around him.

PAUL ZACH
Musician with The Porter's Gate Worship Project

Before reading Dan Marotta's book on the Lord's Prayer, I didn't expect yet another treatment of it could be so theologically deep—insights into the kingdom of God and the problem of evil—and so immediately practical. For serious Bible students and those just beginning to learn to pray, this book is of great value.

SKIP RYAN
Former Chancellor and Professor of Practical Theology at Redeemer Seminary (Dallas)

D. J. MAROTTA

LITURGY
IN THE
WILDERNESS

How the Lord's Prayer
Shapes the Imagination
of the Church in a Secular Age

MOODY PUBLISHERS
CHICAGO

Unless otherwise indicated, Scripture quotations are from the ESV® Bible (The Holy Bible, English Standard Version®), copyright © 2001 by Crossway, a publishing ministry of Good News Publishers. Used by permission. All rights reserved. The ESV text may not be quoted in any publication made available to the public by a Creative Commons license. The ESV may not be translated into any other language.

Scripture quotations marked NASB are taken from the (NASB®) New American Standard Bible®, Copyright © 1960, 1971, 1977, 1995, 2020 by The Lockman Foundation. Used by permission. All rights reserved. www.lockman.org

All emphasis in Scripture has been added.

Published in association with Don Gates of The Gates Group. www.the-gates-group.com.

Edited by Amanda Cleary Eastep
Interior and cover design: Erik M. Peterson
Cover vector art copyright © 2021 by Vadym Ilchenko / iStock Photos (1302770490). All rights reserved.
Author photo: Rebecca Sable Photography

All websites and phone numbers listed herein are accurate at the time of publication but may change in the future or cease to exist. The listing of website references and resources does not imply publisher endorsement of the site's entire contents. Groups and organizations are listed for informational purposes, and listing does not imply publisher endorsement of their activities.

Library of Congress Cataloging-in-Publication Data

Names: Marotta, D. J., author.
Title: Liturgy in the wilderness : how the Lord's prayer shapes the
   imagination of the church in a secular age / D. J. Marotta.
Description: Chicago : Moody Publishers, 2022. | Includes bibliographical
   references. | Summary: "In Liturgy in the Wilderness, Anglican priest D.
   J. Marotta shows how the Lord's Prayer provides a framework in our
   secular age for understanding, believing, and living in light of Jesus
   Christ. With this book, Marotta awakens our hearts to the beauty,
   sustaining power, and bounty of the Lord's Prayer and shows us how to
   live faithfully in the wilderness"-- Provided by publisher.
Identifiers: LCCN 2022010077 (print) | LCCN 2022010078 (ebook) | ISBN
   9780802428561 (paperback) | ISBN 9780802475374 (ebook)
Subjects: LCSH: Lord's prayer--Criticism, interpretation, etc. |
   Christianity and culture. | Wilderness (Theology) | BISAC: RELIGION /
   Christian Living / Prayer | RELIGION / Prayer
Classification: LCC BV230 .M2945 2022 (print) | LCC BV230 (ebook) | DDC
   226.9/6--dc23/eng/20220625
LC record available at https://lccn.loc.gov/2022010077
LC ebook record available at https://lccn.loc.gov/2022010078

Originally delivered by fleets of horse-drawn wagons, the affordable paperbacks from D. L. Moody's publishing house resourced the church and served everyday people. Now, after more than 125 years of publishing and ministry, Moody Publishers' mission remains the same—even if our delivery systems have changed a bit. For more information on other books (and resources) created from a biblical perspective, go to www.moodypublishers.com or write to:

Moody Publishers
820 N. LaSalle Boulevard
Chicago, IL 60610

1 3 5 7 9 10 8 6 4 2

Printed in the United States of America

For Rachel

Our Father, who art in heaven,
hallowed be thy Name
thy kingdom come,
thy will be done,
on earth as it is in heaven.
Give us this day our daily bread
And forgive us our trespasses,
as we forgive those
who trespass against us.
And lead us not into temptation,
but deliver us from evil.
For thine is the kingdom,
and the power, and the glory
for ever and ever. Amen.[1]

CONTENTS

FOREWORD

S even years ago, my life collapsed.

At the time, I was a former missionary who felt called to the field of law. In a matter of months, that missionary became converted to the nervous, medicating lawyer who couldn't sleep for the anxiety and panic attacks.

How did this happen?

With the clarity of hindsight, I see now that I was converted by *habit*. As my friend Dan writes in the pages you're about to read: "It is our embodied habits, not our ideals, that carry the day."

My habits certainly carried my day. They carried even more. My habits of incessant busyness and technology carried me to a place of such existential crisis that my life began to unravel until little but panic and suicidal thoughts remained.

To be sure, I had never before experienced such a wilderness. I hope I never do again. But, alas, I am not the best author of my own life. That was the season when I learned what Dan expresses so well in this wonderful book: that the wilderness is the place of God's transformation. Indeed, He is with us, even in the valley of the shadow of death. It is there that He delivers us from evil. Praise God!

Looking back on that time, I can now say that there was one thing above all else that saw me through that wilderness season: prayer.

Specifically, habits of prayer. Or, if we want to get fancy, *liturgical* prayer.

As it turned out, my life was already shaped by liturgies. It was just the liturgy of inboxes, constant alerts, incessant client responses, and downright anti-human busyness. What I needed wasn't liturgy. What I needed was *better* liturgies.

In short, the manna in my wilderness was the liturgy of prayer.

Through reading the wisdom of other Christians who came before me, through seeking the accountability of friends, and ultimately through the powerful grace of the risen Son of God who worked through all those things, I found that punctuating my day with prayers that were not even my words completely transformed my life.

What I discovered during that wilderness crisis might have been new to me, but it was not new to the church.

It's what the church has known for thousands of years, and it is what Dan Marotta explains so eloquently in this book: *that our habits of prayer shape us.* Far more than we think.

I suspect that you, reader, are also in your own wilderness. It may look like mine; it may look very different. But life is all wilderness, and what you are about to read in these pages will be a balm to your weary soul.

I will bet that before you start this book, you can already recite the Lord's Prayer. But if you're like me, in a real sense, you have *no idea* at all what you are praying when you say those words.

That is the gift of this book.

In delightfully simple language, Dan explains just how radical these short lines of the Lord's Prayer really are.

Pay attention to the subtitle. Because Dan is not just suggesting you learn something new about what Jesus meant by these words. He is asking you to "reimagine" the world as Jesus saw it. That is a far more life changing proposition, and that is exactly the point.

But what a real comfort it is to reimagine the world through the holy imagination of Jesus our Savior.

In reading this book, I realized how dim our cultural imagination is compared to the bright light of Jesus' imagination of His Father's world. It lights up the night! Which is why we should pray His imagination instead of our own.

How urgent, for example, that we reconsider the tender fatherliness of "God our Father." How paradigm-shifting, that we reimagine the comforting authority of "thy will be done." How calming, that we remember the generosity of "daily bread." How earth-shatteringly powerful, that we awaken to reality with the prayer "deliver us from evil." How radical an encouragement, that we remind ourselves that "thine is the kingdom, and the power, and the glory for ever and ever. Amen."

But above all, how practical that the end of this book is not just a new idea, but a new practice: prayer.

So here is my advice: *pray as you read.* This book is a delight, and you could easily consume it quickly. But I urge you, read a chapter and then pray it out. Pray this prayer, thousands of times over if you must.

Because that is the point, not that we become people who understand more, but people who *pray more*. Praying, after all, changes lives.

Lord knows we need it. Literally—Jesus our Lord knew we would be living in the wilderness. So, He gave us this prayer.

Consider Dan like a kind father, who is simply helping you unwrap the gift that Jesus gave us in these wonderful words.

Don't just marvel at the gift. Take it. Go use it. Play with it. Be delighted with it.

It will change you. It did me.

JUSTIN WHITMEL EARLEY
Business lawyer and author of *The Common Rule: Habits of Purpose in an Age of Distraction* and *Habits of the Household: Practicing the Story of God in Everyday Family Rhythms*

INTRODUCTION

You will never get out of the wilderness. Stop trying.

From the first moment you inhale to the last moment you exhale, all your breathing will be wilderness air. Humanity was born in a garden, and it will consummate in a city; but in between lies the wilderness. So many of life's anxieties today are the product of an attempt to escape this in-betweenness, this wilderness tension.

Some look back in nostalgia, pining for a bygone era that felt less wild and unstable than the present moment. *If only we could get back*, they think. Others look forward with determined optimism, setting their hopes on the right combination of education and legislation that promises to put the world right. *If only we could move forward,* they think. Others, scorning the anxious attempts of the political right and left to impose their will on society, seek a different sort of escape. Self-medicated and digitally numbed, they seek only to experience as little pain and as much pleasure for today as possible. Though taking radically different shapes, all are attempts to escape the present moment, pregnant with all its wild uncertainty and danger.

The unsolicited invitation open before you is to embrace your present life in the wilderness and to resist all attempts of escapism: conservative reconstruction, progressive deconstruction, or techno-logically assisted consumer anesthesia.

WILDERNESS IS THE RULE, NOT THE EXCEPTION.

Embracing life in the wilderness also means resisting half measures. You are not in a "wilderness season" that will soon be over if you take up better habits and learn to pray and live the right way. While it has become somewhat fashionable to refer to particularly difficult seasons of life as "wilderness seasons," this is not the way that Scripture and the historic church have understood the wilderness. Rather, wilderness is the rule, not the exception, for the Christ follower's life.

- When Adam and Eve first rebelled against God and fractured the universe, they were cast out of the cultivated garden into the wild, filled with thorns, thistles, and pain culminating in death.
- Noah and his crew boarded the ark and voyaged through forty days and nights of storms, followed by a wilderness of flood waters.
- The Israelites were delivered from slavery in Egypt, traversed the Red Sea, and were led into the desert where they wandered for forty years.
- Jerusalem was sacked by the Babylonians, and the best and brightest of Judah were exiled into a kind of urban, pagan wilderness where they were indoctri-nated in the culture of Babylon.

- Christ, after His baptism in the river Jordan, marched into the wilderness to dwell there for forty days. He took up the vocation of the chosen people of God (faithfulness) in the *context* of the people of God (wilderness).
- Death is the ultimate wilderness. Exiled from the presence of God the Father and life itself, Christ died on the cross and descended into Sheol.
- In the same way, death is the final stretch of wilderness that awaits us all.

It is only after wandering through the wilderness of this life and crossing the threshold of death's door that we may enter the land for which we have been longing, knowing or unknowingly, all our lives. The great sojourn will end as we enter the gates of a city vibrant with life and tranquil with peace. Then, and *only* then, will we leave the wilderness behind. The resurrection of the dead to the glory of the new Jerusalem and a renewed earth marks the end of the wilderness. Therefore, today, in the here and now, the call of God to His church is the call to go with Him into the wilderness and to dwell with Him there while we await the completion of His redemptive work in the world, culminating in the new creation. So, learn to put your hope in the resurrection, and in the meantime, embrace the wilderness.

THE SHAPE OF OUR PRESENT WILDERNESS

Deserts and jungles are both hostile environments, but in different ways. Similarly, each era's wilderness has its own peculiar shape. The primary shape that the wilderness takes in Western societies today is secularism. Difficult to define with any great precision, secularism overshadows our world like an ashy layer of gray clouds, letting in enough light to see around, but blocking any view of sun or stars. Under the low roof of these skies, the air is close and claustrophobic. We become painfully self-conscious, all too aware of ourselves and our beliefs. Under these skies, you are free to believe in the sun or not, but either way, you will be hyper-aware of what beliefs you and others choose. This awareness of choice removes any sense of the givenness or transcendence of the world. Nothing is granted. All is constructed, and therefore, may be deconstructed. This uncertainty, manifested as simmering anxiety, is a hallmark symptom of the secular age. According to the *Washington Post*, over one-third of all Americans now show signs of clinical anxiety or depression or both.[1] This should grieve, but not surprise us. The burden of constructing one's personal identity, meaning, and purpose in life is too great for anyone to bear, and people are beginning to buckle under the weight.

If the first symptom of the secular age is anxiety, the second is a diminished imagination.

In C. S. Lewis's novel *The Silver Chair*, the characters fall under the enchantment of the Lady of the Green Kirtle who rules an underground kingdom. As her intoxicating perfume, and the monotonous thrumming of her instrument, fills the air, she begins to speak in the sweetest of tones words that lull the adventurers into a trance: "There is no overworld. There is no sun. There never was a sun."[2] As the spell takes hold, the characters begin to repeat the words back to her. "There is no overworld. There is no sun. There never was a sun." What is happening?

Their imaginations are asphyxiating. They are coming to believe that the only reality is what they can see around them. The evil witch (for a witch she is) knows that if she can but deaden their imaginations, they will be trapped forever.

From the imagination springs desires; from desires flow actions, which over time wear grooves into habits; from habits develop beliefs that justify; and from beliefs come doctrine. Therefore, if you wish to destroy a faith, strike first not at doctrine; rather, starve the imagination, and doctrine will eventually wither away on its own. Conversely, if you wish to ignite faith, do not begin by teaching doctrine didactically; rather, begin by firing up the imagination. For this, the best kindling is prayer. Prayer is the dry tinder for imagination work because it brings us into conversation with God, the source of all creativity and beauty.

> **IF YOU WISH TO DESTROY A FAITH, STRIKE FIRST NOT AT DOCTRINE; RATHER, STARVE THE IMAGINATION, AND DOCTRINE WILL EVENTUALLY WITHER AWAY ON ITS OWN.**

WHO'S AFRAID OF THE WILDERNESS?

Secular wilderness feels vastly different from, say, the wilderness of Christendom, which some folks will undoubtedly think is a contradiction. But Christendom was indeed yet another long stretch of wilderness for the saints of the church. Embedded and enmeshed with territorial empires, the institutional church fell into heresy, corruption, and rampant injustice.

The brightest lights during the Christendom wilderness were not those who co-wielded the power of empires with kings and queens, but rather those who recognized the dangers of the wilderness and in response embraced a life of living counterculturally: Augustine, Benedict, Francis of Assisi, Bernard of Clairvaux, Julian of Norwich, Teresa of Avila, and their kind. In the same way, if we are to shine as beacons in our secular wilderness, we too must embrace a countercultural life—not one that involves a withdrawal from society, but rather one that actively resists both the temptations and fears of our time, all while actively participating side by side with diverse neighbors in a pluralistic society.

This is hard. Loved by few, hated by many, dismissed by many, traditional followers of Jesus are being pushed to the margins of Western culture and civic life. Since the 1960s, each subsequent generation has become less interested and committed to the Christian faith, and more than two-thirds of the churches in the United States have plateaued or are in decline.[3] While churches were formerly understood to be important institutions for the flourishing of society and promotion of the common good, a growing percentage of the population now views the church as the *enemy* of the good and an impediment to social progress. Biblical beliefs, especially in the realms of gender and sexuality, are now held as irrelevant at best and dangerous at worst.

Committed followers of Jesus today face a future where their very presence is likely to be taken as an existential threat to the health and well-being of their neighbors and cities. As Timothy Keller advises, "Churches in Western Society have to deal with something they have never faced before—a culture increasingly hostile to their faith that is not merely non-Christian (such as China, India, and Middle Eastern countries), but post-Christian."[4] For many faithful followers of Christ, this means a difficult future where pain, suffering, and persecution are likely to become regular experiences.

But although there are very real dangers that incite very real fears, there is absolutely nothing to be afraid of. The voice of the prophet Isaiah was a guide for Israel, and is for us as well, "Fear not, for I am with you; be not dismayed, for I am your God."[5] Rather than telling ourselves that everything is going to be okay and that we stand on the precipice of the next great awakening, or hitting the panic button and sounding the retreat into Christian enclaves, or gearing up for battle, I would like to suggest two seemingly irreconcilable realities:

1. We must dwell in the wilderness of our secular age, and there is no going back. The danger is real. People will get hurt.
2. We may face this danger cheerfully, unfazed, because the Lord is with us.

The church is like a child lying in bed who grows afraid of the dark as the sun sets. As the light fades, we cry out that there are monsters under the bed and in the closet. Our mother comes in to check on us. We want her to either turn the lights back on or tell us that there are no such things as monsters. But we get neither. To our shock, she tells us that there are real monsters who intend to eat us alive and that the lights are staying off. Goodnight. Thanks, Mom.

It's not quite that bleak, though, because she doesn't leave the room. Rather, she continues to sit on the edge of the bed, comforting us with her presence and inviting us to continue to talk with her. This kind of conversation between parent and child in the dark, pregnant with both fear and the invitation to trust, is a picture of prayer.

The God of the Bible does not abandon us to survive the night alone; He waits out the night with us. There is no better picture of a God who comes to dwell in the wilderness with His people than the incarnation of Jesus, the Son of God come to us in human flesh. Jesus shows us why there is no reason to be afraid, no matter how deep and dark and terrifying the wilderness is, because He is present with us. Christ Himself is our consolation, even in the midst of our desolation. He journeys through this wilderness with us. The Scriptures and the church of the past is the experienced voice of a wilderness guide. The saints of the past call to us, "Courage, dear heart!"[6]

THIS KIND OF CONVERSATION BETWEEN PARENT AND CHILD IN THE DARK, PREGNANT WITH BOTH FEAR AND THE INVITATION TO TRUST, IS A PICTURE OF PRAYER.

Navigating this wilderness will require many things from us that are not new to the historic church, but they may feel new to us. We must heed the voice of Scripture and the saints of old, those who have climbed these treacherous mountains before us. Along the way, we will be tempted to reminisce about decades past when following Jesus seemed easier and living publicly as a Christian earned social credibility. But we must resist the temptation to try to re-create the past or to control the future. We must embrace the present.

EMBRACING THE WILDERNESS

Here's how I began to embrace life in the wilderness. The year 2013 was one in which I viscerally felt desolation. My family was living two thousand miles from our nearest relative. My wife and I had few friends, little money, and too much work. I went about my days irritable and stressed. I know I was a bear to be around, not only for my wife and kids, but also for my neighbors. Whenever I encountered people who obviously believed and lived differently from me, I found myself instinctively critiquing, judging, and condemning with a cold heart. I had very little empathy or compassion for others. I was living like a conceited emperor in my own small, twisted Empire-of-Self, and I was at war with the rest of the world. In sum, the gap between what I knew *about* Jesus and how I *embodied the virtues of* Jesus was growing wider by the day.

The lifeline for me came in the form of three men who graciously invited me into their friendship. On Mondays, at 4:00 p.m. at a coffee shop in Littleton, CO (yes, you're right, that's far too late in the day to drink coffee), we would sit and talk about faith, theology, marriage, parenting, elk hunting, Liverpool Football Club, and anything else that might come up. Nothing was off the table. One thing I learned after our third or fourth time together was that each of these men was drawn toward an ancient, liturgical way of following Jesus. This was unfamiliar to me, but as I asked questions, and I learned that we appreciated similar authors, pastors, and books, including *Mere Christianity* by C. S. Lewis, *Basic Christianity* by John Stott, and *Simply Christian* by N. T. Wright. I can't remember who, but at some point, one of us said, "A mere, basic, simple Christian . . . that's all I've ever wanted to be!"

As the weeks passed, they introduced me to the concept of liturgical prayer (by which I simply mean using other people's words). Others had sought to do this in the past, but I wasn't interested. For the first time, I listened because I was desperate. I wanted to be a virtuous man, husband, father, pastor, and neighbor, but didn't know how to get there. Reading books about patience wasn't making me more patient. Listening to lectures about generosity wasn't making me more selfless. Hearing sermons on evangelism wasn't making me care for my atheistic neighbors. I needed a more powerful way to change.

PRAYING LITURGICALLY GOT ME OUT OF MY OWN HEAD AND EMOTIONS AND INTO SOMETHING BIGGER AND BETTER—THE ONGOING REDEMPTIVE WORK OF JESUS IN THE WORLD.

Praying liturgically was profoundly transformative for me. For starters, it gave me something to do when I didn't feel like praying (which was nearly all the time). Using other people's words to pray reframed, for me, what prayer is supposed to be about. What I mean is, it drew me out of my small, hazy, conceited, troubled, anxious, neurotic self and up into the bright, clear world of God and other people. It got me out of my own head and emotions and into something bigger and better—the ongoing redemptive work of Jesus in the world.

This was initially difficult. It felt inauthentic, contrived, fake. Shouldn't I wait until I *feel* genuinely prayerful and spiritual before talking to God? The gentle, but piercingly honest answer from my new friends was, "Dan, your authentic self may not actually be all that great."

It was devastating to hear at the time, but it was true. I had been letting my worst inclinations lead my spiritual relationship with God, instead of the best practices of wise saints of the past. It was like a bucket of cold water to the face to hear that maybe, just *maybe*, my emotions shouldn't always be allowed to drive the train.

Praying liturgically began to shape me from the outside in, and then, from the inside out. I noticed (and, even better, my family noticed!) that I was softening, becoming just a bit kinder, just a bit more patient, just a bit more interested in other people. At the time of this writing, it has been eight years of learning to pray this way, and in hindsight I can look back and observe the ways that liturgical prayer has changed me. In particular, reciting the Lord's Prayer is what has most transformed who I am. The Lord's Prayer is, after all, the original liturgical prayer for a follower of Jesus.

The Didache, written sometime before AD 300, is the oldest Christian writing outside of the New Testament. Something of an ancient Christian catechism, it contains short instructions on prayer, such as:

> Neither pray as the hypocrites; but as the Lord commanded in His Gospel, thus pray: Our Father who art in heaven, hallowed be your name. Your kingdom come. Your will be done, as in heaven, so on earth. Give us today our daily (needful) bread, and forgive us our debt as we also forgive our debtors. And bring us not into temptation, but deliver us from the evil one; for yours is the power and the glory forever. Thrice in the day thus pray.[7]

From this we understand that Christians in the first centuries of the church were being discipled to navigate the wilderness of their time by praying the Lord's Prayer three times daily, patterned after the Jewish hours of prayer: morning, noon, and evening. These brothers and sisters lived in a fearful wilderness age before the legalization of Christianity. Their wilderness, much like that in parts of present day Myanmar, China, India, and Afghanistan, was not the simmering anxiety of secular pluralism and marginalization, but the choking fear of torture and death. How did they pray? What sustained their faith? At least part of the answer was to continuously pray the Lord's Prayer.

THIS IS THE CARDINAL RULE OF WILDERNESS SURVIVAL: IT IS OUR EMBODIED HABITS, NOT OUR IDEALS, THAT CARRY THE DAY.

The Greek poet Archilochus is thought to have said that under pressure, "We do not rise to the level of our expectations, we fall to the level of our training."[8] This is the cardinal rule of wilderness survival: it is our embodied habits, not our ideals, that carry the day.

Therefore, if you wish, as I do, to become a person of virtue and good cheer as we sojourn through the wilderness, then we must give ourselves to the practices and habits that will shape us at the core of our being. Through both the Old and New Testaments and all of church history, the most fundamental practice for spiritual formation is prayer, and the most fundamental prayer is the Lord's Prayer.

My hope for you, the reader, is twofold.

Personal: First, I hope that, through reading this book, you are struck by the immense value and weight of the Lord's Prayer. I hope that you take up praying it daily and that it becomes an anchoring practice in your life as you walk your pilgrim way through the wilderness. I hope it subverts the idols of your heart—that place where you are tempted to believe that your life is basically about you, your desires, and your comfort. I hope it transforms you from outside in, over time making you into a wiser, kinder, and more joyful follower of the Lord Jesus.

Cultural: Second, I hope that through reading this book you begin to reimagine the world around you. I hope that trust replaces fear, contentment replaces jealousy, and that you start to see enemies through the compassionate eyes of Christ. I hope the Lord's Prayer not only changes your character, but also the way you see the wilderness—where you and I both must learn to follow Jesus while rubbing shoulders with many who do not.

In order for these two things to happen, you need the words of Jesus in the Lord's Prayer to sink down deep into the roots of your soul. In the depths of your being, this prayer will go to work on your desires and imagination—the most fundamental things that make you *you* and determine how you see and engage the world. There, allow the words from the mouth of Jesus to quietly work on you. Trust that it is for your good.

CHAPTER 1

THE NEED FOR SUBVERSIVE IMAGINATION

Beauty is subversive. Why? Because it is powerful. It is powerful because it makes us dream. It makes us think. It makes us imagine a world that is bigger than the one we know and one that's worth taking a risk for. Even in a brutal world, beauty exists and its power leads us to faith, hope, and love.
–MICHAEL FRYER

D r. Pat Brown was not interested in starting a business. As a tenured professor of biochemistry at Stanford University, Pat already had his dream job. But there was something that had bothered him for decades. As a committed vegan, he had long considered the use of animals for food to be the world's greatest environmental problem. So, when he took a sabbatical in 2009, he decided to dedicate the rest of his life to doing something about it.

First, he did the expected thing and organized a conference to raise awareness of the problem. He hosted a National Research Council workshop titled "The Role of Animal Agriculture in a Sustainable 21st Century Global Food System." Not surprisingly, hardly anyone attended. Pat realized that if he wanted to fundamentally change what foods people ate, he was going to have to do more than cite facts and demand change; he was going to have to create a vegetable product that actually *tasted* as good as meat. He realized the path to the change he wanted to see was not through debate or politics or education, it was through *taste*.

> All the facts in the world don't move the needle on public policy; what you have to do is something more subversive. You can't persuade people by education or nagging to change their diet significantly ... look at how well people follow nutrition recommendations for their own health as opposed to the good of the world! ... Public policy doesn't work, education doesn't work—you need a more subversive solution.[1]

IF YOU WANT TO SEE REAL TRANSFORMATION, YOU CANNOT ATTACK PEOPLE'S BELIEFS HEAD ON. RATHER, YOU MUST UNDERTAKE THE SLOWER, RISKIER, COSTLIER WORK OF SUBVERSION.

Pat went on to found Impossible Foods Inc., and in 2016, his "burgers" appeared on menus in restaurants across the country.

Now, your feelings on food ethics aside (I personally enjoy pit-smoked Texas-style brisket, please and thank you) the point of the story is that if you want to see real transformation, you cannot attack people's beliefs head on. Rather, you must undertake the slower, riskier, and costlier (but in the long run, more effective) work of subversion.

This is the change in posture that wilderness Christians must adopt in the twenty-first century. What ought to be the posture of the people of God when they no longer wield cultural power and have become a marginalized fringe group? There are three normal responses to which many of us default, and the purpose of this book is to propose a fourth and better way forward.

THREE NORMATIVE POSTURES[2]

Defensive: In this "shield" posture, an individual Christian, church congregation, or network of churches rightly perceives the potentially corrupting influence of secular neighbors and culture, but wrongly responds out of fear, retreating and insulating themselves from those neighbors and culture.

Passive: In this "white flag" posture, an individual Christian, church congregation, or network of churches rightly perceives the intimidating power and force of secular neighbors and culture, but—due to either disinterest or a sense of helplessness—wrongly responds to such force with apathy or surrender.

Aggressive: In this "sword" posture, an individual Christian, church congregation, or network of churches rightly perceives the threat of secular neighbors and culture to the open practice of Christian faith, but, in anger, wrongly responds with a threat of its own.

Though this is bordering on gross oversimplification, experience bears out that most Christians in Western society fall somewhere in these three basic postures. They either:

1. Feel fearful and want ways to protect themselves and those they love
2. Feel helpless and just go with the flow
3. Feel angry want to take what they feel is rightfully theirs

Of course, there are exceptions, and my guess is that, in reading this, you are not satisfied with these categories.

Good. Neither am I. Let's find a better one.

THE FOURTH WAY IS SUBVERSIVE

Now, if you are a Christian, you might feel the word subversive is inherently negative. It may bring up images of Cold War–era spies or terrorist cell groups. However, at least for the purposes of this book, I'd like to posit that subversion is simply a non-direct way of undermining a system in order to establish something different in its place. Subversion is not a retreat to safety, nor is it peace, nor is it attack; it is a different way of engaging altogether.

- When the United States puts a Starbucks in the Forbidden City in Beijing, that is subversion.
- When Hollywood puts out yet another movie where the Christian character is an idiot, that is subversion.

- When football player Colin Kaepernick kneels during the national anthem, that is subversion.
- If you'd prefer a less controversial example: when a mother says to her child, "Let's pretend we're dinosaurs and eat this broccoli together!" that is subversion.

Consider how each of these is a non-direct way of accomplishing a purpose.

The US doesn't argue for capitalism in China, it just offers fast, convenient coffee.

Hollywood doesn't say "God does not exist," it just makes people who hold that belief look dumb.

Colin Kaepernick doesn't run for political office; he sparks a national conversation.

The creative mother doesn't detail the nutritional information of broccoli, she uses the child's love of play to hijack their resistance to vegetables.

Subversion.

The Most Powerful Method of Transformation

There is no method of transformation—whether for something as small as a personal habit or as large as an empire—more powerful than subversion. Consider these examples...

In 1882, Jigoro Kano invented the physical and moral pedagogy that we now call the martial art of judo, which means "the gentle way." Isn't it interesting to name a method of combat "gentle"? Kano explains:

> In short, resisting a more powerful opponent will result in your defeat, whilst adjusting to and evading your

opponent's attack will cause him to lose his balance, his power will be reduced, and you will defeat him. This can apply whatever the relative values of power, thus making it possible for weaker opponents to beat significantly stronger ones.[3]

A judo master is one who can fluidly turn her opponent's attack against him. She doesn't block his punch; she grabs his wrist and pulls him forward *as* he punches, using his punch to throw him off balance. She doesn't attack her opponent to win, she wins by subverting his attack.

CHRIST DYING ON THE CROSS WAS THE MOST MASTERFUL ACT OF SUBVERSIVE COMBAT.

We might say that Christ dying on the cross was the most masterful act of subversive combat: Satan attacks God to put Him to death. God fluidly uses that attack to overthrow both Satan and death in a single move.

Here's a less violent way of thinking about it: How does every romantic comedy begin? We meet a character who, for some reason, has sworn off dating. What happens next? He comes face-to-face with a woman who is just perfect for him, and we (the audience) know that he will (after much angst) end up with her in the end.

Now, let's ruin this "meet cute" moment with in-depth analysis. What, exactly, is going on when the character who has sworn off dating meets the person they're going to end up with?

- Have their convictions about the evils of dating changed?

- Have their beliefs about the virtues of the single life changed?
- Speaking of change, has anything about them changed at all?

No. Absolutely nothing has changed inside of them. So, what happened to cause the change?

Beauty happened.

It may have come in the form of a stunning supermodel or in the form of an adorably bumbling nerd, but something *arresting* happened, and it subverted all their supposed convictions and beliefs. This is the subversive power of beauty:

> Moments of beauty—be it music, art, nature, or an act of kindness—can take you out of a space of weary familiarity. Beauty, in whatever form it takes, can interrupt a pattern of behavior or a way of thinking and cause us to stop in our tracks and take notice of it.[4]

When beauty meets belief, beauty wins every time. Why? Because belief attempts to persuade your mind with data and doctrine while beauty skips past your brain and goes right to your heart, your gut, and your instincts.

THE SUBVERSIVE WAY OF JESUS

The gospel of Jesus set forth in the Bible is also subversive, though we may not be accustomed to thinking of it that way. When God took on human flesh in the person of Jesus, entered our world as a baby, lived the life that we could not live, died the death we deserve to die, rose to new life as a guarantee of our future resurrection, ascended to heaven to reign on the throne, and sent His Spirit to dwell in our hearts, that was subversion. How so? If we take the apostle Paul's words in Romans 5 and 8 and the pain and suffering of our world seriously, then we must admit that humanity has made itself an enemy of God. So, what kind of posture does God take toward a hostile world?

Defensive?	Retreating to heaven and barring the gates to keep wicked humans out?
Passive?	Blithely watching our downfall and shrugging it off as our problem, not His?
Aggressive?	Reconquering the world by force?

Each of these postures occur on some level in the biblical story. God does *defensively* maintain the purity of heaven in His divine presence, and sinful humans enter it at their peril, as the prophet Isaiah experienced when he found himself drawn into the throne room and cried out, "Woe is me! For I am lost; for I am a man of unclean lips."[5] God does—in seeming *passivity* for a season—allow us and the world to go our own way. As the psalmist writes, "Awake! Why are you sleeping, O Lord? Rouse yourself!"[6] God does, at times, *aggressively* use force, as Pharaoh discovered in Exodus chapters 7 through 14. But, while God does adopt these postures in limited ways for limited periods of time, His primary posture toward hostile humanity is benevolently subversive. God does

WE MUST ADMIT THAT HUMANITY HAS MADE ITSELF AN ENEMY OF GOD. SO, WHAT KIND OF POSTURE DOES GOD TAKE TOWARD A HOSTILE WORLD?

not fundamentally defend from, ignore, or attack His enemies; He loves them and, at the cross, dies for them. Why? To win former enemies over to Himself that He might dwell with them in peace. The good news of the gospel is inherently subversive in nature.

Subversive Stories

Not only did Jesus embody God's subversive love, but Jesus also told subversive stories. Have you ever wondered why the parables of Christ are *still* so effective after all this time? It is because these ingenious little stories have a way of burrowing into our brains and slowly transforming us from the inside as the meaning gradually dawns on us.

For example, take Jesus' parable of the great banquet in Luke 14. Jesus is reclining at a table with Pharisees and other spiritual heavyweights. Things must have been going well because one of them says, "Blessed is everyone who will eat bread in the kingdom of God!"[7] Though the language is strange to our ears, this is exactly the sort of thing you or I might say if we had the chance to share a meal with Jesus in our lifetime. The man is having a grand time. He's essentially saying, "This meal we're sharing together with You, Jesus, is a taste of heaven!"

And Jesus, in response, tells a story about a man who gives a great banquet and invites his friends. His friends make excuses and don't show up. So, the master sends servants to instead invite the poor, crippled, blind, and lame, and then to go out to the highways and hedges and bring everyone in so that his house will be filled for the party. The story harshly concludes with the master declaring that the original invitees will never enjoy the banquet. What has Jesus just done? He's told a story that has obvious internal consistency, but that doesn't appear at first to have anything to do with what the excitable man has just said. However, upon closer examination, you realize that the story actually has *everything* to do with the man's enthusiastic statement. Jesus is saying, Yes. Blessed are those who eat bread in the kingdom of God, *but those people are not who you think they are.* They are not those religious elites who think they're on the invite list; they are the outcasts and strangers whom no one would expect to see at the banquet table.

How is this subversive? The truthfulness of a parable is self-evident. It's only later that you realize it applies to you and requires you to change; but by then it's too late! You already believe it! Now you are faced with the uncomfortable, but potentially transformative, reality that you believe something that is obviously true and yet does not jive with your current life. Congratulations. Thou hast been subverted.

THE LORD'S PRAYER

And so, when Jesus' disciples asked Him to teach them to pray and He gave them a handful of words to pray that summarize the entirety of what it means to be His follower, that was subversion.

The Lord's Prayer is inherently subversive, for at least three reasons:

It is liturgical.

At first blush, praying a liturgy can feel like an exercise in the worst of rote, ritualistic religiosity (try saying that three times quickly!). *Making my mouth say the sounds doesn't mean that my heart is alive to God.* Quite right. But have you considered that all our relationships begin with learning to repeat other people's words? We teach our infants to relate to their parents by saying "Mama" and "Dada." When a beaming new father leans over the crib and whispers, "Can you say Dada?" he is essentially doing the same thing as a newly baptized Christian learning to say, "Our Father." Liturgy establishes relationship non-directly, subversively.

I serve as a priest in an Anglican church. When our congregation gathers for worship, I don't begin the service with a long lecture on how we are all one, united church family; rather, we simply begin praying liturgically together. No doubt many of us are entering the room feeling somewhat disconnected, both from God and from each other. But if we are willing to move our mouths and pray the liturgy in unison—trusting the Holy Spirit to work—then we often find that somewhere along the way our hearts have genuinely and authentically come alive both to God and to each other.

If liturgical prayer in a church worship service is strange and foreign to you, think about it this way: Why do great crowds of people love singing together at concerts? Why do wild throngs of fans love to chant together at major sports games? Is it because we all showed up with equally high levels of loyalty for the band or team? Absolutely not. I bet there are a lot of lukewarm first-timers in the stands. But if there is a vibrant, powerful singing/chanting/shouting-in-unison aspect to the concert or game, then we first-timers are going to find ourselves *loving* that band or team. Why? Because the communal liturgy subversively shapes

COMMUNAL LITURGY SUBVERSIVELY SHAPES OUR AFFECTIONS BY SWEEPING US UP IN A POWERFUL EXPERIENCE.

our affections by sweeping us up in a powerful experience.

The Lord's Prayer works on the same principle. It subversively shapes our affections because it is a liturgical prayer.

It is deceptively short and simple.

No doubt the disciples expected Jesus to give them a complex, long-winded dissertation on the nature of prayer and the proper forms and rules of prayer. He gave them none of that. Rather, He gave them a simple framework that is still recited two thousand years later. The simplicity and brevity of the Lord's Prayer is part of the subversion. We hear it and think, "This seems easy enough." We may even be tempted to think it so short and simple that it's boring and we need to move on to bigger, better, longer prayers. This would be a grave mistake. The Lord's Prayer is something like the wardrobe in C. S. Lewis's Chronicles of Narnia. It's bigger on the inside than it is on the outside. After a while we end up thinking, "Is there anything that is *not* contained in this prayer?"

It goes to work on you.

When a Christian prays the Lord's Prayer, they are reciting (and hopefully remembering) what this following Jesus business is all about. The prayer has a reciprocating effect of shaping the person who prays it. As you pray the words, you are reminded that this is what you believe, and so you believe a little deeper. As you believe a little deeper, your actions begin to align just a bit more closely with your beliefs. There's an ancient Latin phrase that Christians have used through the centuries that summarizes this effect: *Lex Orandi, Lex Credendi, Lex Vivendi*, the Law of Praying is the Law of Believing is the Law of Living.[8] What you pray shapes what you believe shapes how you live. Another way to say it would be: prayer subverts your life.

This is a profoundly biblical conception of discipleship. The world was, after all, formed by words. God speaks all creation into existence. Christians not only believe this, but also believe that the Word of God became flesh and dwelt among us in the person of Jesus. Since we are so word-created and word-centered in our doctrine, should we not also be word-led in our discipleship? I must let the words lead and hope that my sluggish heart will catch up.

WHAT YOU PRAY SHAPES WHAT YOU BELIEVE SHAPES HOW YOU LIVE.

RENEWED IMAGINATIONS THROUGH PRAYER

Christians are in desperate need of renewed imaginations today. The future of the church in Western society appears to be one of an exhausting struggle in a secular wilderness where spiritual imaginations are stifled and in danger of dying altogether. We cannot rely on the old imagination of a culture that once shared some (not all) Christian morality. We cannot (and should not) place our hopes in retreating to personal piety, or blending in, or in winning a culture war. Rather, we must begin to imagine life as a faithful and fruitful minority that is ever seeking to subvert what is evil with good, what is hateful with love, what is corrosive with nurture. A crucial first step toward living this reimagined life is praying and practicing the Lord's Prayer. Therefore, each of the following chapters will explore a phrase of the Lord's Prayer by asking:

1. What is the prayer inviting a person to pray, believe, trust, and do?
2. What personal and cultural factors make this particularly difficult or impossible?
3. How does the gospel beautifully subvert this aspect of life in such a way that praying and living becomes possible for us?
4. How might we begin to reimagine the world through this prayer?

CHAPTER 2

REIMAGINING GOD AS SHARED

The way we are, we are members of each other. All of us. Everything. The difference ain't in who is a member and who is not, but in who knows it and who don't.

–WENDELL BERRY

You don't choose your family, they are God's gift to you, as you are to them.

–DESMOND TUTU

OUR Father, who art in heaven,
   hallowed be thy Name,
   thy kingdom come,
   thy will be done,
     on earth as it is in heaven.
Give us this day our daily bread.
And forgive us our trespasses,
   as we forgive those
     who trespass against us.
And lead us not into temptation,
   but deliver us from evil.
For thine is the kingdom,
   and the power, and the glory,
   for ever and ever. Amen.

The opening invocation of the Lord's Prayer seems a bit of a false start. The collective pronoun "our" immediately challenges what I think I know. I think I know who I am and who God is. I think I have a decent grasp of who the good guys and the bad guys are out there in the big scary world. And when it comes time to talk to God, I think I know what I need. However, the Lord's

Prayer tells me I am wrong on every point. Thankfully, in God's kindness, He does not slap my folded hands or roll His eyes in annoyance. Rather, like a patient parent whose child has just burst into the kitchen demanding a snack, God smiles at me and gently says, "Let's back up and try that again, shall we?"

This may be the best way to understand the tone of Jesus' voice when His disciples ask Him to teach them to pray and He responds, "When you pray, say."[1] It was expected for first century rabbis to teach their disciples proper technique in prayer; and thus, the disciples' request was not an unusual one. Of course, not much has changed in two thousand years. People continue to ask pastors, rabbis, shamans, and gurus for advice on prayer technique, and all too often, we vendors of spiritual goods and services are eager to dispense our wisdom of the mysteries of the universe. Two things are true here:

1. Books proposing to offer a brilliant, secret, new way of praying will always be top sellers.
2. Those same books will soon line the shelves of Goodwill thrift stores.

My offer to you, the reader, is not a new, hitherto undiscovered form of praying that will unlock the treasures of divine pleasure, as if God were a cellophane-wrapped candy bar whose sweetness you could enjoy if only you could just find that invisible edge of the plastic and start pulling. Rather, the audacious idea here is to offer something that is not new, but old, and not secret, but public. The Lord's Prayer is very old and very well-known. Case in point, people who openly mock the church have the Lord's Prayer memorized. Clearly it doesn't work very well.

Or does it?

G. K. Chesterton wrote, "The Christian ideal has not been tried and found wanting, it has been found difficult, and left untried."[2] In the same way, I propose that the Lord's Prayer has not been prayed and found ineffectual; it has been found unimpressive and left un-prayed.

> **I PROPOSE THAT THE LORD'S PRAYER HAS NOT BEEN PRAYED AND FOUND INEFFECTUAL; IT HAS BEEN FOUND UNIMPRESSIVE AND LEFT UN-PRAYED.**

Therefore, the intent of this book is to impress upon us all the ways in which the Lord's Prayer subverts our understanding of who we think we are, who we think God is, what we think of our lives in this world, and what we need. Of course, this marvelous prayer from the lips of Jesus has been doing just that with people for two millennia, but a few of us (namely, me) have missed it.

Let's begin.

OUR

This is one of those funny situations where you're only lost if you're paying attention. Our? Why the plural? Who is included in this "our"?

From the crack of the starting pistol, we have already gotten into trouble with this prayer. It's like trying to follow directions that begin with, *Step 1: Combine said ingredients.* We think we must have missed a step and begin shuffling through stacks of papers looking for the lost front page. Most of us naturally fall into two camps: those who would like to address God as "*My*

God" and those who feel more comfortable with a respectfully distanced "Mr. God, sir."

The "*My* God" people like praying. They feel cozy with God. He's like that fantastic third-grade teacher who would wink at you when the rest of the class didn't understand the lesson, but you both knew that *you* did. There's something wonderful about being this sort of person. You get the approachability of God. You love that God is always available, always present, always ready to listen. You feel like a child of God, and the next word in the prayer, "Father," flows naturally off your tongue.

The "Mr. God, sir" people generally do not like praying. They prefer for the pastor or priest to do their praying for them. There's something wonderful about being this sort of person as well. You get the awful, terrifying otherness of God. You respect that God is beyond you and therefore shouldn't be approached too casually. God is not a golden retriever, and you know it. God is more like a Clydesdale draft horse. Entering his field is dangerous, you might get a hoof through your skull. To use the biblical metaphor, God is like a lion and prayer feels like entering His territory. Better to leave such dangerous work to the professionals.

For both types of people, that little word "Our" may trip them up. "Our" tells you that God is neither your God, nor is He someone else's God. He is not private or borrowed; He is shared. The plural "Our" immediately shows us that prayer is not a one-on-one conversation between us and God, it involves other people.

Who are these other people? Well, given that we're about to address God as "Father," the logical answer would be that all the children of God are included in the "Our." As the beloved disciple John wrote, "But to all who did receive him, who believed in his name, he gave the right to become children of God."[3] The Anglican Catechism puts it succinctly:

Q: Why does Jesus teach us to pray "our" Father?

A: Jesus teaches us always to understand ourselves not only as individuals but as members of God's family of believers, and to pray accordingly.[4]

So there. The "Our" is all the children of God. "Our" sets us in a family. Easy enough, right? Maybe not. For many, there's something offensive about the word "Our." When we slow down and think about who all might be included in this, we start to get uncomfortable. If we dwell on it too long, we may even break out in hives. Personally, there are people I find rather obnoxious, and I'd rather not pray with them. I may even get uncomfortable thinking about the fact that *I* am included in that "Our." Groucho Marx may have had the church in mind when he said, "I don't want to belong to any club that will accept me as a member."[5] After all, the children of God are an unruly bunch and not exactly known for their virtue: "'Ah, stubborn children,' declares the LORD, 'who carry out a plan, but not mine.'"[6] When the disciples considered who all might be included in this "Our," no doubt they squirmed. Could the "Our" include: Prodigal sons and elder brothers? Tax collectors and prostitutes? Pharisees and Roman soldiers? Rich young rulers and impoverished widows?

In our current cultural moment, could the list of deplorables read: Christians of other denominations and tribes? Liberals and conservatives? Activists and passivists? Urbanites and country folk? People who listen to Nickelback? Millennials and Boomers?

No doubt you can easily think of a few people who shouldn't be allowed in, who shouldn't be allowed to use "Our." The "Our" is fundamentally offensive because it places us in the same category as people we have spent our entire lives working very hard to differentiate ourselves from. After all the time, money, and energy I've put into becoming the "right kind of person," the "Our" tells me I'm just going to get lumped in with the flotsam and jetsam of the church! I'm glad to pray *for* those who have somehow managed to make their way into the church, but do I have to pray *with* them? Do I have to identify with them? The answer from the Lord Jesus is a quiet, warm, and simple "yes," which at first feels disappointing, but which bears within it a wonderful privilege. Jesus is a part of the "Our."

When we say "Our," we are not only put into the gang of illegitimate children of God, but we are also put into siblinghood with Christ, our older brother. The Lord's Prayer invites us to address God in union with Jesus Himself. If we would pray with Jesus, then we must pray with His people—all of them—even (and perhaps especially) with those we don't much like. This is why, if a congregation embraces the practice of praying the Lord's Prayer weekly in corporate worship, it provides a means by which people of differing political and cultural convictions can move toward unity in Jesus. It might not hold the disparate groups together forever. But if all understood the radical "Our" that was coming out of their mouths, they would at least experience a weekly reminder that there can

THERE CAN BE NO PRIVATE ACCESS TO JESUS THAT DOES NOT INHERENTLY INCLUDE A FAMILY RELATIONSHIP WITH OTHER SINNERS.

be no private access to Jesus that does not inherently include a family relationship with other sinners.

Jesus looks out on His disciples who are hungry for the best way to pray, thirsty for a way of praying that will give them a spiritual leg up in the world. Jesus perceives the same tendency toward a competitive, judgmental, and spiritual consumerism in them that He rightly perceives in us. But He does not sigh with exasperation. Rather, like that patient parent from earlier, He thinks, "Let's back up and try this again, shall we?" When you pray, say "Our..."

"Our" subverts our preferences and assumptions about who is in and who is out. Jesus doesn't tell us that we're wrong or give us a detailed list of who's in or out. He simply instructs us to say "Our" with Him, leaving it to us to reflect on who else might be saying "Our" as well.

QUESTIONS FOR DISCUSSION

1. Are you more inclined to think of God as yours or someone else's?
2. Who else is included in the "Our" that you may not have previously realized (or desired)?

PRAYER FOR MEDITATION O HEAVENLY FATHER, You have seen fit to place me into Your family alongside brothers, sisters, fathers, and mothers in the faith. Give me, through the redeeming work of Jesus, the charitable eyes to see both myself and Your followers rightly, so that with patience, grace, and unity, I may participate, through the Spirit, in the worship, work, and fellowship of Your people. Amen.

CHAPTER 3

REIMAGINING GOD AS AFFECTIONATE

Our **FATHER**, who art **IN HEAVEN**,
hallowed be thy Name,
thy kingdom come,
thy will be done,
on earth as it is in heaven.
Give us this day our daily bread.
And forgive us our trespasses,
as we forgive those
who trespass against us.
And lead us not into temptation,
but deliver us from evil.
For thine is the kingdom,
and the power, and the glory,
for ever and ever. Amen.

Coach Boone: Are your parents here?

Gerry Bertier: Yes.

Coach Boone: Good. [nods his head at Gerry's mom]

Coach Boone: You take one last good look at her. Cause once you step on that bus you ain't got your mama anymore. You got your brothers on the team and you got your daddy. You know who your daddy is, dontcha? Gerry, if you want to play on this football team, you answer me when I ask you who is your daddy? Who's your daddy, Gerry? Who's your daddy?

Gerry Bertier: You.

Coach Boone: And whose team is
   this, Gerry? Is this your team? Or
   is this your daddy's team?
Gerry Bertier: Yours.
Coach Boone: Now get on the bus.
   Put your jacket on first, and get on
   the bus.
–REMEMBER THE TITANS, 2000

Most people have an allergic reaction to the idea of calling God "Father." As I write this, it's April in Richmond, Virginia, which means the air is choked with yellow pollen dust. When the pollen is released from the trees and bushes, it travels in great, swirling clouds that descend to blanket cars, porches, and (if you foolishly left your windows open, as I did last night) the faces of your sleeping children. I knew spring had arrived when my kids woke up with red, itchy eyes and stuffy noses. This is what it feels like for many people to be told to address God as "Father." It triggers our histamines; it makes us uncomfortable for at least two reasons:

First, we may have personal, emotional baggage with the word "Father." Half of us come from homes that have been broken by divorce, and the majority of us who have lived through that pain went with our mothers and not our fathers. A significant percentage of children of divorce grow up feeling not the presence of a loving father, but rather the absence of an estranged father.

And those of us who did grow up with a dad in the house, even a great dad (worthy of a World's Best Dad coffee mug), still have experienced pain, disappointment, and hurt because of our fathers. In fact, father wounds are so common they are considered by some experts to be a "normative developmental trauma."[1]

> The difficult . . . relationship leaves a deep impression
> . . . which is manifested in myriad direct and disguised
> forms of desperately seeking some contact, some
> closeness with one's father (or his surrogate), or in being
> furious at him for his failures. Many . . . are burdened
> with feelings that they never knew their fathers, nor how
> their fathers felt as men, nor if their fathers even liked
> them, nor if their fathers ever really approved of them.[2]

I can tell you, as someone who holds a psychology degree in family therapy and as a dad with four young children, it is terrifying to think about the way that my failures will impact my own children, as they undoubtedly will.

But must the sin and failure of our earthly fathers be a barrier to our addressing God as our Father? No, and in fact the pain and hurt we've experienced from our earthly fathers should actually be the very thing that points us back to God as Father. Here's why: none of us has ever had a perfect dad. Every single human being post–Adam and Eve—from Cain, to Jesus, to you—has had a sinful human father. And yet, none of us has *ever* gotten used to it. Sinful fathers are a universal human condition; they are a changeless feature of societal landscape, as predictable as death and taxes, and yet we still know deep down that it shouldn't be that way. And that is a clue. It shows us that we were *meant* to have a good father.

SUBVERTING THE PATRIARCHY

Things are going to get more complex before they get better because there are broader, cultural problems that arise when we are invited to address God as Father. The second reason we struggle with calling God "Father" is that it causes many women (and some men) to wonder if this is yet another way of participating in literally thousands of years of male oppression. When the Christian Scriptures instruct you to address God as "Father," are you upholding and participating in the patriarchy?

[Note: In this instance, the word "patriarchy" is being used as a summative word for societal concern over male dominance to the detriment of women. The technical, historic definition of "patriarchy" has more to do with the rule of a father over the household, including wife, children, servants, etc.]

Regardless of whether you share this concern, there's actually some surprisingly good news here for everyone. When Jesus invites you to address God as Father, He's not only *not* participating in a culturally oppressive patriarchy, He is subverting it. Here's how: In first century Rome, Caesar held the title "Father of the Empire." If you lived in the first century and someone asked you the question: Who is "our father"? The "proper" answer would've been, "Caesar." Additionally, first-century Roman family culture was dominated by the *pater familias*. The male head of household ruled over the money, the resources, and even the smallest details of the lives of his wife, children, and servants.

If you think the word Father is emotionally charged today, it carried even *more* political and familial weight in the first century! And Jesus, by deliberately inviting you to begin praying to God as Father, is subtly but powerfully communicating two things: 1) that Caesar is not your father, and 2) even the *pater familias* is not your father (more about this later). So you see, to address God as Father is not a form of participating in a culture of oppressive patriarchy; it's actually subversive to all oppressive forms of patriarchy by subtly undermining the claim to dominance and replacing it with something better—the authority of God, who is neither male nor female.

When the early church prayed "Our Father," it probably gave Caesar fits, and it presented a thrice daily dose of humility to any male head of house that might be tempted to think he could rule over women, children, and servants with impunity. In this way, "Our Father" began to quietly but powerfully undermine and transform the twin empires of government and family. There is something timely here for us because, though the specifics have changed, the alluring power of these two empires remains.

SUBVERTING CHRISTIAN NATIONALISM

For two years I had the privilege of serving at a church in northern Virginia with deep roots that predate the founding of the United States. In fact, George Washington was a member of the Parish Council.[3] I have fond memories of my time with that wonderful congregation, and I confess it gave me a special affection for Washington, whom many call "the Father of Our Country." I have learned tremendously helpful truths about leadership from the stories I heard about him and wish I had half the courage of that great man.

However, one of the dangers that arises from knowing some of the virtues of the founders of the United States is the temptation to blend faith and patriotism into Christian nationalism. American followers of Christ should be wary of this for two reasons:

1. It has never worked anywhere, ever.
2. Jesus specifically taught against it.

Anytime the church gets in bed with the government, an illegitimate child is conceived. History contains the long, sad story of God's people learning, forgetting, and relearning this over and over again. The allure of political power is enticing for Christians because it presents itself as a shortcut to realizing the kingdom of God.

> **THE ALLURE OF POLITICAL POWER IS ENTICING FOR CHRISTIANS BECAUSE IT PRESENTS ITSELF AS A SHORTCUT TO REALIZING THE KINGDOM OF GOD.**

Why engage the slow, painful process of loving our enemies when we could just make our enemies' beliefs (or existence) illegal?

While allegiance with political power initially seems expedient, it always, *always* turns against the church. If you will indulge a bit of Anglican church history (forgive me, I'm a priest), I think the reality of this statement will become apparent. Henry VIII ordered the beheading of Thomas More for refusing to acknowledge him as the supreme head of the Church of England. Mary I (whom we not-so-affectionately call "Bloody Mary") oversaw the 1555 Oxford Martyrs of Nicholas Ridley, Hugh Latimer, and Thomas Cranmer for refusing to recant their reformed theology. (Neither Catholics nor Protestants are innocent here.) Switching gears, the more recent complicity of the German National Church in the early twentieth century during Adolf Hitler's rise to power should be sufficient to caution Americans against the dangers of Christian nationalism.

But that is merely (merely!) the lesson of church history. Now for the real kicker, Jesus Himself taught against the marrying of faith with political power.

> Again the devil took him to a very high mountain and showed him all the kingdoms of the world and their glory. And he said to him, "All these I will give you, if you will fall down and worship me." Then Jesus said to him, "Begone, Satan!"[4]

> "Show me the coin for the tax." And they brought him a denarius. And Jesus said to them, "Whose likeness and inscription is this?" They said, "Caesar's." Then he said to them, "Therefore render to Caesar the things that are Caesar's, and to God the things that are God's."[5]

> Jesus answered, "My kingdom is not of this world. If my kingdom were of this world, my servants would have been fighting..."[6]

Christ our Lord did not directly address politics very often, but when He did, His message was consistent: "Do not confuse what I came to do with earthly, political power. Do not confuse kingdom work with empire-building."

We may not be accustomed to thinking of the Lord's Prayer as politically charged, but it is. "Our Father" is a politically subversive invocation—it was in the first century, it continues to be so today. In a subtle, non-direct manner, the prayer aligns our allegiance with God and, therefore, away from political fathers. Caesar doesn't want you praying the Lord's Prayer, and most politicians of *any* country today don't want you to either.

Which, of course, is why you should.

SUBVERTING THE IDOLATRY
OF THE NUCLEAR FAMILY

Moving a bit closer to home, the "Our Father" phrase also sub-verts the idolatry of the nuclear family. There are two kinds of empires you know. There is the great, grand, glorious empire *out there;* and there is the private, quiet-but-fiercely-defended empire *in here.* The empire within takes a variety of forms in dif-ferent cultures, but in the United States, it often takes the form of prizing the ideal nuclear family above all else. Despite the on-going gender and sexual revolution, for the majority of people in Western culture, squad goals remain essentially the same: marriage, kids, house, dog (optional), vacations, school, college, weddings, grandkids, family reunions, big funeral. Bonus points if, along the way, you manage to get a multigenerational family picture in matching white polo shirts on a beach.

Now, lest you think I've descended into snarky deconstruc-tionism, you should know that I am describing *my* family—whom I adore. The point is not to devalue the goodness of a healthy, thriving nuclear family but rather to poke fun at the reality that this vision has, for some, ascended to the throne and reigns on high. Which means that some followers of Christ may be privately tempted to imagine that the purpose of their faith is to serve their family life goals. How can you tell if this has hap-pened to you?

Here is a simple diagnostic question: If you had to choose between having a happy, successful family where everyone has nominal faith or a suffering, struggling family where everyone's faith is so deep it's the only thing holding them together, which would you choose?

If you're anything like me, you're mostly annoyed at the question. But our annoyance reveals something in us, doesn't it? We don't want to choose between happiness and suffering, or between success and struggle. We desperately want to believe that we can have fantastic faith *and* all worldly success at the same time. We want to gain the whole world without losing our soul. The "Our Father" will have none of this. The "Our" plucks us right out of our family beach picture and drops us into the awkward group photo of our local church. We look around and instead of the American Dream Family we see what often looks more like a raft of refugees recently washed up on the shore.

SOME FOLLOWERS OF CHRIST MAY BE PRIVATELY TEMPTED TO IMAGINE THAT THE PURPOSE OF THEIR FAITH IS TO SERVE THEIR FAMILY LIFE GOALS. HOW CAN YOU TELL IF THIS HAS HAPPENED TO YOU?

The "Father" dethrones the parent as head of house and establishes God as the leader of the family. Of course, many Christians believe all this in a kind of abstract, theological sense. The real friction occurs when "Christianity" is taken out of the realm of theory and lands with a thud next to us as "The Church." And not just "The Church!" universal and global with trumpets, but rather "Your Local Church" with untuned pianos and pastors in pleated khakis pants with coffee breath.

It's easy for Christians to identify with the grand doctrines of the Christian faith and yet not identify with their local church. But this ex-carnational mindset is part of the problem. It allows us to idolize our nuclear family, which feels "real," and give lip service to belonging to the church in a spiritual, global, historical sense, which (for most people) feels "unreal." The scandalous *realness* of the local church is part of the subversive invitation of "Our Father." It reframes the way we see the people around us. They are not fellow attenders; they are brothers and sisters, uncles and aunts, grandparents, nieces, and nephews. This is glorious good news for both the marrieds and singles, the parents and the childless. It tells the marrieds with children: you are part of something so much bigger than you own little nuclear family project. Your children are, first and foremost, not yours, but children of the church. It tells the singles and the couples struggling to conceive: you are not isolated, you are not childless, you are part of a real family!

So whether we are tempted toward a form of Christian nationalism or nuclear family idolatry, the opening invocation of the Lord's Prayer pulls the ugly carpet right out from under us, knocking us to our knees and revealing beautiful oak floors we didn't even know were there. This is a much better place to be.

OUR WOUNDS REVEAL OUR NEED

I told you it was going to get more complex before it got better. Now it's time for things to start looking up, because the weakness and wounds and baggage that we all carry with the word "father" are meant to reveal the deep and abiding hunger that we have for a true Father.

- A Father who is compassionate, gentle, and patient
- A Father who doesn't lose His temper
- A Father who doesn't get bored and check His phone when you're talking
- A Father who is interested in you, who finds your

thoughts and feelings and ideas and problems
fascinating and wants to hear more about them

- A Father who is present and doesn't keep leaving to
go do other things that are more important than you

Now, I want to home in on that last one: a father who is *present*. One of the most important questions many people ask as they face the wilderness of their lives is, "Where is God in all this?" And the Lord's Prayer gives us the answer in the first line: God is in heaven; or, if we translate the Greek literally, the God who is "in the heavens."

IN HEAVEN

Now we misunderstand this without even trying because we, through no fault of our own, have had our imaginations shaped more by Hollywood than the Scriptures. The cinematic version of heaven goes something like this: A blank, white space with no dimensions. No up or down, right or left. People in flowy white linen clothes. Some old guy (perhaps Professor Dumbledore or Morgan Freeman) is there to explain to newbies how heaven works. There is no sense of time or purpose. We are left to assume that an eternity of boredom is better than the vision of hell as pan-seared human flesh (also from Hollywood). Because our imaginations have been so shaped by the box office, when we pray "Our Father in heaven," our brains automatically conjure up images of God as Gandalf and heaven as some undesirable place of mind-numbing disinterest. It is surely a galaxy far, far away.

This makes the majority of Christians in Western society into functional deists. By this I mean that though we may not profess a doctrine of God as a watchmaker who winds up the world and walks away to observe from a distance, we certainly default to living as if this is exactly what we believe. We go about 99.8 percent of our lives as if we are alone in the cosmos and it is up to us to scratch out a living for ourselves on this blue planet. And then, every so often, we remember, "Oh yeah, God! Prayer!" And we ask for Him to do something for us. Pleading for Him to come down from wherever He is up there and get involved for a moment, fix our problem, and then go back to leaving us alone. We are all the disciples in the boat on the Sea of Galilee: "Jesus, we're sinking!" If God were the German coastguard, He might reply, "Vhat are you sinking about?"[7] He is *in* the boat, y'all. That is the meaning of "in heaven." God is in the boat with us, even if we cannot see Him.

And so, here we are in desperate need of renewed imaginations. "In heaven" is not code for far away; in fact, it's the *opposite*! Heaven is not up. Heavens, no. It is the dimension of this world that our physical senses cannot perceive. It is the unseen, spiritual realm that is the other side of the coin of the "seen" and experienced physical realm. When Jesus says God is "in the heavens," He doesn't mean God is distant; He means, quite literally, the opposite: God is near. Because He is in heaven, He is near. If we used theological language, we would say that God is "immanent." He is right here with us—Immanuel.

If we pray and believe in the immanence of God, then it should be a tremendous comfort to us. Even when we suffer in debilitating isolation, we are never alone *because* God is in heaven. When we are separated from our loving relationships and miss the warmth of our friends' and family's presence, God's immanent presence is our comfort because it the presence of a loving Father—tender and gentle and merciful. As the psalmist writes, "As a father shows compassion to his children, so the LORD shows compassion to those who fear him."[8]

When you pray, you are speaking to the most compassionate, affectionate being in the universe who is also in the room with you, who is as near to you as your own thoughts.

Our Father in heaven.

PUT YOUR JACKET ON & GET ON THE BUS

One of our family's favorite movies is *Remember the Titans*. We feel a special connection to the movie because my parents grew up in the northern Virginia public school system around the same time as the partially true events the film is based upon. When Coach Boone (played brilliantly by Denzel Washington) is preparing to take his newly integrated high school football team off to Gettysburg College for pre-season training camp, he is confronted by All-American Gerry Bertier. The white student athlete tells the new black coach how the team is going to be run. And Coach Boone, demonstrating a remarkable level of self-control and emotional intelligence, does not argue with him. Rather, he asks him a hilariously embarrassing and subversive question, "Who's your daddy?" Faced with the new reality that playing for his team means submitting to the new coach, Bertier wisely mumbles, "You." Coach Boone follows it up with another question, "Is this your team, or is this your daddy's team?" Again, Bertier, deflated, answers, "Yours." With authority firmly established, Coach Boone instructs him to put on his jacket and get on the bus. While we don't know it at the time, later we will learn that this interaction is filled with genuine affection. As the story plays out, Coach Boone will become something of a father to these boys.

What I love about that interaction is that it charts the course for the following story arc of the team going to camp. There will be tension over who is in charge. Who will define who is in and who is out? What does the team really need going forward? If there had been a false start, the prospects of the team might have ended right there in the parking lot.

So it is with us and God. As we begin, we need the opening invocation of the Lord's Prayer to orient us, to firmly establish God in His role and us in ours. There is no epic journey together until we get that sorted out. God is our Father. He chooses the family, not us. He's stunningly majestic, and yet He is right here with us. His tender affection for us is our comfort.

We're off to a good start.

QUESTIONS FOR DISCUSSION

1. What sort of images does the word "Father" stir up in your imagination?
2. What sort of images does the word "heaven" bring to mind? How does a clearer understanding of the biblical use of the word heaven change the way you pray this part of the Lord's Prayer?

PRAYER FOR MEDITATION LORD GOD, I confess it is difficult to call You Father and to believe that You are near. Help me, through the sacrifice of Christ, to know Your tender love for me and for all Your children. Send the Holy Spirit to comfort me with Your presence. Kindle in my heart the affection of Your love so that I may be warmed by Your Fatherly fondness and respond with sincere, childlike devotion. Amen.

CHAPTER 4

REIMAGINING GOD AS BEAUTIFUL

Beauty will save the world.
–Fyodor Dostoevsky

Oh, taste and see that the LORD is good!
–Psalm 34:8

Our Father, who art in heaven,
HALLOWED BE THY NAME,
   thy kingdom come,
   thy will be done,
      on earth as it is in heaven.
Give us this day our daily bread.
And forgive us our trespasses,
   as we forgive those
      who trespass against us.
And lead us not into temptation,
   but deliver us from evil.
For thine is the kingdom,
   and the power, and the glory,
   for ever and ever. Amen.

Nobody really likes the word "hallow." It's an old word, and there isn't a contemporary English equivalent, so the translators of the Bible were forced to keep using the old word. Hallowed means: sacred, sanctified, made holy, and separate. "Hallowed be thy Name" means that God's name, God Himself, is to be the most sacred, special, honored, worshiped person in the entire world. To pray "Hallowed be thy Name" is to say that there is no one like God, that nothing in this world can compete with the value, goodness, worth, and beauty of God Himself.

Now, this seems pretty straightforward. This is the kind of

stuff we expect from the Bible—worshiping God, right? But wait, there is a subtle subversion taking place here. You see, the human reality is that we all hallow something. It might be a person, job, image, money, reputation, or sexual appeal. We all have things in our lives that are of greatest value to us. There are not two kinds of people in the world: hallowers and non-hallowers. There is only one kind of person: the hallower, the worshiper.

The plain fact is that most of our prayers tend to fall in the category of asking God to hallow what we hallow, to value what we value; instead of hallowing and valuing Him. The majority of our extemporaneous prayers take the form of supplication (making requests of God). And our supplications are often focused on things we want that we don't have, or things we have that we don't want.

- God, please help me get _____ job.
- God, please help my kid do better in school.
- God, please heal my friend's disease.
- God, please give me a boyfriend/girlfriend/ husband/wife.

Lest you think I'm a coldhearted monster, I have prayed *all* of these prayers many times. But I recognize in myself a dangerous habit: I am not immune to making career, kids, health, and romance into the most desirable, important thing in my life. I am liable to hallow them. And so, if I'm not careful, my well-intentioned extemporaneous prayers might well run counter to the prayer that Christ taught us.

Jesus is subverting our worship. Jesus is taking what He knows our prayers tend to orbit and is flipping it around. Jesus knows that we have a tendency to approach God with a list of wants. He is saying that, instead, we ought to pray that what we want more than anything is God Himself.

CRISIS REVEALS WHAT YOU HALLOW

You see, what you pray about in a time of crisis reveals what you hallow. Whether losing a job, going through a bad breakup, or receiving a cancer diagnosis, a crisis is like a rototiller grinding up the soil of our lives and exposing the insides to daylight. Many of us find that there are far more worms, rocks, and weeds buried in us than we thought. When we pray, we expose what we care about the most. So I ask you, in your time of crisis, what do you pray about?

- Are your prayers primarily for yourself or for others?
- Do your prayers tend to orbit your own needs, your own desire for safety and comfort?

Prayers in crisis reveal what we value most, and valuing *anything* more than God is not only idolatrous, but also devastating to your well-being. When God lays out the first commandment, "You shall have no other gods before me," He is not only establishing a spiritual law, He also has our best interests at heart. It is a *kind* law. In other words, idolatry is like methamphetamine; it's not only illegal, but also straight up bad for your health. The apostle Paul writes about the incompatibility between idolatry and God in one of his letters to the church in Corinth.

> What agreement is there between the temple of God and idols? For we are the temple of the living God. As God has said:

"I will live with them and walk among them,
    and I will be their God,
    and they will be my people.
Therefore, go out from their midst,
    and be separate from them, says the Lord,
    and touch no unclean thing;
    then I will welcome you,
    and I will be a father to you,
    and you shall be sons and daughters to me,
says the Lord Almighty."[1]

The apostle is quoting from the Old Testament books of Leviticus, Isaiah, and 2 Samuel, where God repeatedly instructs His people to have a singleness of heart, to focus their worship and affection on Him and not attempt to divide their hearts between God and idols.

The reason for this is that God is not just one of many things that we might love. God is not one item on the menu, one spiritual good on the shelf. God is holy, other, different. He is in His own category. Allowing your desire for a lucrative career to compete with your desire for God is like allowing your desire for a grande frappé to compete with your desire for a spouse: "I feel within myself a deep, existential hunger and finding a good husband sounds too complicated. I'll satisfy this craving with seventy-two grams of sugar in a coffee-flavored milkshake." It's like choosing a fedora over a home: "I feel exposed, vulnerable, homeless, and adrift in this world and houses are expensive. I'll make do with this hat." The difference in order of magnitude is absurd. There is *nothing* that is like God. All metaphors (especially mine) eventually break down. All analogies fail in the end.

God is separate and distinct from every atom of creation, and comparing His value to the value of something in the created world is a sin against both God *and* the created order *and* each other *and* ourselves. Consider the fallout of such comparison:

It wrecks our relationship with God: We are made in God's image to reflect His goodness and beauty to the world in stewardship, and to reflect the world's goodness and beauty back to God in worship. When we place something other than God as our greatest treasure, we fracture the most important, fundamental relationship we have.

It wrecks our relationship with the world: When the relationship between humanity and God is severed, the world becomes like a cut flower in a vase. It still looks lively, but separated from the source of life, it is slowly dying. Incapable of eternal renewal, the materials of the world become scarce resources.

It wrecks our relationship with others: Remove one parent and the family unit breaks down. Estranged from the Father, the people of God fall apart. We come to view each other as competitors for the scarce resources of the material world.

It wrecks our relationship with ourselves: Separated from God, living in a dying world populated with hostiles, we come to view ourselves through the lens of competitive strengths and weaknesses. No longer are we each beautiful image bearers, we are either sexy or ugly. No longer are we each uniquely gifted to bring about the flourishing of world, we are either talented or below average.

Novelist David Foster Wallace, in his famous commencement address at Kenyon College, described the destructive capacity of misplaced worship:

> In the day-to-day trenches of adult life, there is actually no such thing as atheism. There is no such thing as not worshipping. Everybody worships. The only choice we get is what to worship. And the compelling reason for maybe choosing some sort of god or spiritual-type thing to worship—be it [Jesus Christ] or Allah, be it YHWH or the Wiccan Mother Goddess, or the Four Noble Truths, or some inviolable set of ethical principles—is that pretty much anything else you worship will eat you alive. If you worship money and things, if they are where you tap real meaning in life, then you will never have enough, never feel you have enough. It's the truth. Worship your body and beauty and sexual allure and you will always feel ugly. And when time and age start showing, you will die a million deaths before they finally grieve you. . . . Worship power, you will end up feeling weak and afraid, and you will need ever more power over others to numb you to your own fear. Worship your intellect, being seen as smart, you will end up feeling stupid, a fraud, always on the verge of being found out.[2]

While certainly not speaking from a place of faith in Jesus, Wallace has tapped into groundwater truth: anything or anyone you worship, other than God, will eat you alive.

This is why God will suffer no competition. He is not motivated by pride, but love. As a good parent, He is not content to let us leave home to go live with the family of cannibals. As a good spouse, He will allow no abusive rival lovers. He is not selfish; rather, He understands the universe that He has created better than we do. He knows that when human beings give Him their ultimate love and value, they will live with the grain of the universe and flourish. On the other hand, if they give anything other than Him the place of ultimate value, they will flounder and perish in shame and heartbreak.

> **GOD WILL SUFFER NO COMPETITION. . . . AS A GOOD PARENT, HE IS NOT CONTENT TO LET US LEAVE HOME TO GO LIVE WITH THE FAMILY OF CANNIBALS. AS A GOOD SPOUSE, HE WILL ALLOW NO ABUSIVE RIVAL LOVERS.**

Therefore, in giving us the Lord's Prayer, God insists that we cannot pray to Him as an intimate, immanent Father unless we *also* value and worship Him as transcendent Lord.

In order to pray as a follower of Jesus, you must hold the immanence of God and the transcendence of God together. God is near and He is holy. He is *both* the still small voice whispering to your soul, *and* He is the mighty creator who wills the universe into existence.

THE PROBLEM

Now you may think: "I can't do that. I can't hold both of those together. If I really believed that God was transcendent and mighty and powerful and that He suffers no rival, I would be afraid to talk to Him. I can't approach God with intimacy and safety if I must also see His majesty. I can have one or the other but not both."

And a lot of people default to this kind of thinking. A lot of people choose one or the other. They choose the gentle, intimate God who is always there to listen, but they balk at the transcendence and majesty of God. And so, God becomes their therapist. They like God the way they like a good counselor. But that kind of relationship is marked by affection without respect. And since they do not respect God, they feel free to reject His commands the way they feel free to reject the advice of a pay-by-the-hour therapist. This is sometimes (not always) the same kind of person I mentioned earlier who would like to pray, "*My* God."

Other people choose the transcendence of God. They choose the all-powerful, almighty, sovereign God. They look down on mystics who talk about God as a lover. They don't understand those people. They admire God from afar and they do not, *cannot*, experience intimacy with God because, in their heart of hearts, they fear God, and fear eventually turns into resentment. This is sometimes (not always) the same kind of person I mentioned earlier who is inclined to pray, "Mr. God, sir."

Christian prayer is having the boldness to walk into the temple of the sovereign God as if you were walking into your living room. It's having the respect to know that you shouldn't lead with a whiny wish list, and yet having the level of comfort to know that it's perfectly appropriate for you to begin with, "Good morning, Dad." How could anyone have that kind of audacity and intimacy?

We can have this kind of audacity and intimacy because

of the one who is teaching us to pray. Jesus is the transcendent God come near. In Jesus, the immanence of God and the transcendence of God meet and become one in the incarnation. If we were to use a math equation, we might say: Immanence + Transcendence = Incarnation.

The Son of God, the second person of the Holy Trinity, becomes a walking, talking, eating, sweating human being. In Jesus, the transcendence (the mighty, awesome, holy, otherness) of God comes near to us; but not to strike fear into our hearts or to judge us, but rather to give Himself for us—to die for us, so that we can approach God as Father and hallow Him above everything else.

IMMANENCE + TRANSCENDENCE = INCARNATION

If all this feels a bit ethereal and intangible for you, you're not alone. This is why God has given His people the sacraments, so that we might have tangible means of engaging Him.

The Subversive Beauty of Water

It rained last night in Richmond, and this morning there are little rivulets of yellow pollen swirling in pools on the sidewalk in front of our home. The air is clear for the first time in days, and the sky is piercingly blue. This is what baptism does for us—provides clarity and the capacity to breathe deeply—only more so. United with Jesus by the water of baptism in His death and resurrection, we can now approach God as Father. This is possible because through Jesus' death, which pays the penalty for our sin, and through His resurrection, which secures our future, we are adopted into God's family with Jesus as our older brother and God as our Father.

> "In Christ you are all sons (and daughters)[3] of God through faith."[4]

> "See what kind of love the Father has given to us, that we should be called children of God; and so we are."[5]

Through the water of baptism, we former-frappé-drinking, fedora-wearing orphans can begin to hallow the Father above everything else. Once we understand what He has done for us, the kind of love He has for us, we could never desire anyone or anything else more than God Himself.

The Subversive Beauty of Bread & Wine

If David Foster Wallace were still alive today, a follower of Christ might respond to his insightful commencement address with a simple reversal. What sets Jesus apart from all other gods and idols is that He is the only one who says, "Instead of me eating you, you must eat me."

WHAT SETS JESUS APART FROM ALL OTHER GODS AND IDOLS IS THAT HE IS THE ONLY ONE WHO SAYS, "INSTEAD OF ME EATING YOU, YOU MUST EAT ME."

This is what makes the worship life of the church not only a little different, but the complete inverse of all other forms of worship. Instead of bringing our offerings, we receive Christ's offering. Instead of sacrificing to our God, our God sacrifices for us. Instead of worshiping something that will consume us, we worship a God that invites us to consume Him. What a beautiful, arresting mystery! It should stop us dead in our tracks every week. Whenever we see a loaf of bread and cup of wine on a Communion table, we should be dumbstruck, "I can hardly believe that this is how much God loves us . . . it's beautiful."

SUBVERTING THE EMPIRE

The first lines of the Lord's Prayer subvert our personal and cultural empires, big and small, a fresh understanding of who God is and what He is like:

- OUR: subverts either private ownership of God (my) or fearful distance from God (your), with the intimate, yet communal, "Our."
- FATHER: subverts our personal wounds and our cultural concerns with compassionate authority.
- IN HEAVEN: subverts our functional deism with transcendent nearness.
- HALLOWED BE THY NAME: subverts our little idols with astonishing beauty.

He is not my private God or someone else's borrowed God. He is both a gentle Father and a holy Lord. He is immanent and transcendent. Through the wonder of the gospel, we can hold all these together because they are held together in Jesus. And when we do, we discover that God is more wondrously beautiful than we previously imagined.

REIMAGINING THE CHURCH
IN THE WILDERNESS

When we pray "Our Father in heaven, hallowed be thy Name," how do you and I begin to reimagine what it means to be the church journeying through the wilderness of our time?

With these words on our lips, we begin to imagine that:

- We are already a part of a big, rambunctious family that needs us just as much as we need it. We belong.
- We are not orphans destined to limp through life because of our wounds. Rather we are loved, adopted, and cherished by the Father we always knew we were meant to have. We are wanted.
- God is not distant, but near and present with us. We are not alone.
- We live in a world where God is not just available to comfort us, but is of such beauty and value that He transcends every other good thing in our lives and becomes our ultimate good. We are lovestruck, enraptured.

We belong. We are wanted. We are not alone. We are in love.

With these words on our lips, we begin to subjectively believe what is already objectively true: that God has brought His holiness near to us in Jesus and has given Himself for us that we might be brought near to the Father. With these words on our lips, we begin to believe the gospel. And as we begin to believe the gospel, we begin to *embody* the gospel—words transforming our thoughts and desires which, in turn, transform our actions. If God is my Father, what is there to fear? Certainly not pandemics, or liberals, or conservatives, or immigrants, or debt, or being alone, or any of the other myriad spooks that want me to cower in fear.

If God is hallowed above all else, what thing of ultimate value could be taken from me? Nothing. With these words on our lips and minds and hearts, our lives begin to take on the kind of courage and confidence that is only possible for a true child of God.

QUESTIONS FOR DISCUSSION

1. Imagine a coffee table in your home. On it are placed all the things you hallow the most. What is on the table?

2. How would you describe the difference between the old imagination and a new imagination offered by these lines of the Lord's Prayer: *"Our Father in heaven, hallowed be thy Name"*?

PRAYER FOR MEDITATION BELOVED CREATOR, You alone are the object of my desire, but I have chased after lesser loves. Unveil to me the wonders of Your beauty in the person and work of Jesus that, with fresh eyes, I may behold in You both the source and consummation of all my longings. Grant me, by Your Spirit, a single-minded passion to hallow You above all else. Amen.

CHAPTER 5

REIMAGINING GOD AS GOOD

"Our kingdom go" is the necessary and unavoidable corollary of "thy Kingdom come." For the more there is self, the less there is God.
-ALDOUS HUXLEY

Our Father, who art in heaven,
hallowed be thy Name,
THY KINGDOM COME,
THY WILL BE DONE,
ON EARTH AS IT IS IN HEAVEN
Give us this day our daily bread.
And forgive us our trespasses,
as we forgive those
who trespass against us.
And lead us not into temptation,
but deliver us from evil.
For thine is the kingdom,
and the power, and the glory,
for ever and ever. Amen.

O ne of the interesting (and perplexing) challenges of our current cultural moment is that God's demonstrated goodness has become a prerequisite for His existence. What I mean is, the question "Is God good?" has become far more important to people than "Is God real?" This has not only become the primary challenge of Christian evangelistic witness and cultural apologetics, but it has also become the central task of discipleship and spiritual formation, both for children and adults. The zeitgeist of our time is not so much interested in philosophical debates on the logical, rational existence of a divine being, but rather evaluating the God of the Bible by one's personal moral standards.

DEFINE "GOOD"

The problem with asking a seemingly simple question like, "Is God good?" is that it immediately begs a much harder question, "What do you mean by '*good*'?" If we are honest, our gut response might be something like, "By good, I mean God is on my side." We imagine that, if God exists at all, surely He must be a bigger, stronger, more powerful version of ourselves. He generally likes the things that we like. He disapproves of the things (and people) we disapprove of. God "gets" it the way our close friends "get" it. Of course, if we had to say that out loud we would immediately recognize the absurdity of it. As Voltaire is attributed to have written, "In the beginning God created man in his own image, and man has been trying to repay the favor ever since."[1] The problem is, if you don't believe in a God who can disagree with you, you don't believe in a God at all.

GOD'S DEMONSTRATED GOODNESS HAS BECOME A PREREQUISITE FOR HIS EXISTENCE.

COLLISION OF DESIRES

The next line of the Lord's Prayer forces us to reckon with the dilemma that God's agenda might be different from our own. Can we believe in a God who wants something different than what we want? Could that even be a good thing? There is a great collision happening here. It's the smashup of our will versus God's will, our desires versus God's desires. If that image seems violent, you're not wrong. It *is* violent. Desires and wills do not go gently into that good night—they rage. This line may very well be the wildest and most terrible prayer that will ever escape our lips.

IF YOU DON'T BELIEVE IN A GOD WHO CAN DISAGREE WITH YOU, YOU DON'T BELIEVE IN A GOD AT ALL.

For that reason, it is a true wilderness prayer. Let's explore it.

KINGDOM?

So what exactly is the kingdom of God? When we hear the word kingdom, what images come to mind? What did Jesus' contemporaries imagine when they heard that word? If you asked a first century Jew what the kingdom of God was, you would have received a very concrete answer. They would say, "Look, the kingdom of God will come when a new Moses arrives to drive out the Roman Empire so that we can inhabit our own land and dwell in freedom. The kingdom of God will be a second exodus, a revolution, a conquering of one empire and the establishment of another." The first century Jews would have conceived of the kingdom of God in cultural, political, and even militaristic terms.

And you can't blame them for thinking that way. Anyone who has ever lived under an oppressive regime usually begins to pray and hope that God will deliver them by overthrowing their enemies.

CONFUSION ABOUT THE KINGDOM

Jesus' teaching and ministry was surprising and counterintuitive for most people. Think about John the Baptist. He establishes a thriving ministry proclaiming to people that the kingdom has arrived in the Messiah and calling people to prepare their hearts and bodies by repenting and being baptized. All was going well, until the government turned on him, and John the Baptist was thrown in jail where he knew he would likely be executed. This was not the kingdom he expected. So, he sent some of his followers to go find Jesus and they asked him, "Are you the one who is to come, or shall we look for another?"[2]

I find this so very comforting. Scripture describes John the Baptist as the *greatest* human who ever lived aside from Jesus Himself,[3] and *even* John the Baptist did not recognize the kingdom of God being established right before his eyes! Perhaps you and I can be forgiven for being a bit fuzzy on what exactly is the kingdom of God.

Do you know how Jesus replied to his question? "The blind receive their sight and the lame walk, lepers are cleansed and the deaf hear, and the dead are raised up, and the poor have good news preached to them. Blessed is the one who is not offended by me."[4]

The kingdom of God that Jesus came to establish was sprouting up all around them, but few had eyes to see it because they were expecting something else: something strong, something fast, something inspiring.

Therefore, at the onset, we must acknowledge that there are plenty of people today who conceive of the kingdom of God in similar ways. There are some who think the kingdom of God will come when the right person is elected as the president of the United States, or when everybody goes to church, or when Christian culture is the dominant culture, or when the enemies of Christianity are defeated. On the other hand, some folks may be put off by this kind of language, and so any talk about the kingdom of God is, initially, troubling.

We might be worried that the kingdom of God basically takes the shape of colonization and cultural imperialism in which one culture comes in and suppresses another culture. Does the kingdom of God mean a version of Christian culture (do you imagine Western European/ American culture?) dominating and eventually eradicating all other cultures? Does it mean an end to the wide variety and diversity of human cultures on earth? We must be clear, right at the beginning, that the kingdom of God is *not* the establishment of one culture or class as normative for all, but rather the *renewal of all cultures.*

THE KINGDOM OF GOD IS NOT THE ESTABLISHMENT OF ONE CULTURE OR CLASS AS NORMATIVE FOR ALL, BUT RATHER THE *RENEWAL OF ALL CULTURES*.

In his book *Whose Religion Is Christianity? The Gospel Beyond the West*, African scholar Lamin Sanneh writes: "Christianity helped Africans to become renewed Africans, not re-made Europeans."[5] The kingdom of God doesn't suppress cultural diversity, it renews it. This is the vision of the new creation that we see in the book of Revelation: a multiracial, multicultural kingdom, people from every tribe, tongue, and nation gathered in worship. And it's worth noting that no other religion or system of beliefs has this vision—the manifold peoples and tribes of the world renewed and dwelling with diversity, yet harmony; existing as multicultural, and yet peaceful, is a *uniquely* biblical vision.

WORKING DEFINITION OF KINGDOM

So, we need a better working definition for the kingdom of God. Let's try this: the kingdom of God is where God's will is enacted in every sphere of life: spiritually, emotionally, politically, economically, socially, vocationally, etc.

Therefore, "thy kingdom come" equals "thy will be done on earth as it is in heaven." The two phrases are definitions of one another. As the laws of physics govern the cosmos, bringing order to chaos and making possible the flourishing of life, so the will of God is meant to govern our lives, kindle our imaginations, and capture our affections.

> AS THE LAWS OF PHYSICS GOVERN THE COSMOS, BRINGING ORDER TO CHAOS AND MAKING POSSIBLE THE FLOURISHING OF LIFE, SO THE WILL OF GOD IS MEANT TO GOVERN OUR LIVES, KINDLE OUR IMAGINATION, AND CAPTURE OUR AFFECTIONS.

Of course, there is an enormous Grand Canyon–sized gap between this description and our lived experience. Not only does so much of life feel frighteningly random and cruel, but many of us also feel a great deal of frustration with ourselves. We can't escape the gut feeling that the world is not what it should be and *we* are not who we should be.

And so, as we tap into our fears and frustrations and confusions about the world and about ourselves, we may become very curious about this kingdom of God idea. What exactly is it? It is better or worse than our desires for the world and for ourselves? Is this line in the prayer something that you and I can genuinely pray?

PART 1: THE TWO REALMS OF THE KINGDOM

Is the coming kingdom of God primarily an inward, spiritual change or an outward, societal transformation? When we read about how Jesus described the kingdom during His ministry, it can be a little difficult to tell what He means. Sometimes it seems He is describing something inward.

> Being asked by the Pharisees when the kingdom of God would come, he answered them, "The kingdom of God is not coming in ways that can be observed, nor will they say, 'Look, here it is!' or 'There!' for behold, the kingdom of God is in the midst of you."[6]

In this interaction, it appears that the kingdom isn't something we can see, smell, taste, hear, or touch.

But consider Jesus' answer to John the Baptist when John's disciples ask if Jesus is the Messiah or if they should expect someone else. Jesus replies that the blind see, the deaf hear, the poor have good news—these are *all outward, physical manifestations*. It appears Jesus also considers the kingdom to include something that can be observed, something visible.

So which is it? Inward or outward? Personal piety or common good?

The First Realm: Personal Piety

The first realm we might call the realm of personal piety: salvation and sanctification. In this realm, the gospel functions as the good news that Christ died for human sin, and, through the power of His Spirit, we grow in sanctification, becoming more and more the people we were originally made to be. In this realm, the kingdom comes as we put our faith in Jesus, are saved from sin, and then grow to become virtuous people. We learn to obey God, to tell the truth, to be people of integrity, to exercise self-control, to pray, and to study Scripture.

- **What's right?** There is something right about this view of the kingdom: it does include a personal realm. Human beings really are sinful, and Christ really did come to rescue us from our sin and restore us to fellowship with God, so that we fulfill our creational intent by becoming people of goodness, beauty, and truth.
- **What's wrong?** But there is something missing in this view; the picture is incomplete. The kingdom of God is within us, but it is not merely within us. The gospel takes into account not only human guilt, but also the corruption of the world. When the first humans sinned, not only was the human race estranged from God their Father, but also the entire creation was overcast by the shadow of sin. Every fiber of the world became corrupted and is dying a slow death.

You might imagine that human sin is a rock thrown through a stained glass window. The death of Christ deals with the rock: it pulls it back. This rock will break no more windows. But if you leave the gospel story there, you haven't yet cleaned up the mess. There are still shards of glass everywhere. That is the corruption of the world: the breakdown of the family and of society; the rise of racism, economic oppression, cruelty, war, rape, sex trafficking, and drug abuse.

And the kingdom must deal with that as well.

Some of us feel the pain of this world so deeply and see the injustice so blatantly that we can only conceive of the kingdom in physical, societal terms.

The Second Realm: The Common Good

And so, some people conceive of the kingdom of God as primarily a societal kingdom—the realm of the common good—where God's will is justice and mercy for all who are oppressed.

- **What's right?** Now what's right about this? This view takes seriously the outer ministries of Jesus: the healing of the sick, the feeding of the hungry, the ministry to the poor, and the dignifying of the shamed.
- **What's wrong?** However, this view doesn't feel the weight of personal human guilt and so fails to connect sin against God to the plight of the world. To use our stained glass window illustration: the kingdom as "realm of the common good" deals with the shards of glass, but not the rock.

TREATING BOTH SOURCE & SYMPTOMS

Years ago, before my wife, Rachel, and I were married, we served as college summer interns at our home church. During that summer, we led a high school camping trip to Shackleford Banks, a nine-mile spit of land just off the southern coast of North Carolina. One afternoon, Rachel accidentally stepped on a sharp piece of driftwood and cut her foot. In the following forty-eight hours, the wound became infected and troubling red streaks began working up her leg. Soon she could no longer put any weight on the foot. Without any medical training, we thought treating her symptoms (blood and pain) with a Band-Aid and ibuprofen would suffice. It wasn't until we made it back home and she went to see a doctor who properly cleaned the wound that the infection healed and the pain subsided.

Think of sin as the deadly infection and the blood and pain as the corruption of the society. Both require attention. Cleaning the infection without seeking to reduce the pain is heartless medicine. But treating the symptoms without addressed the infection could prove fatal. Both are required, and a good doctor knows this.

In the same way, a faithful follower of Jesus must consider both the realms of the personal and the common good when they pray and labor for the coming kingdom of God. We must hold these two together. We must become people who place our faith in Jesus, are saved from sin, who grow in sanctification, who have a rich and vibrant inner spiritual life; *and* we also must labor for the common good, leveraging our resources and occupations and relationship and networks (not for our own advancement) but for the good of other people who are in need.

Now, you might be thinking at this point, "How do I do this?" After all, while *both-and* sounds a lot more appealing than *either-or*, it is infinitely more difficult. Believing this is one thing, embodying it is quite another. How can this work for us?

The answer lies in the first half of that word kingdom. You see the personal and the common good, the realm of individual salvation and sanctification and the real of societal flourishing, come together under the King who rules both. Kingdoms have kings, and kings rule everything.

Now comes the hard part. We've examined the two realms of the kingdom, and now we must face the offense of the kingdom.

PART 2: THE OFFENSE OF THE KINGDOM

As my friend and neighbor Josh Gibbs likes to say, "The Kingdom of God is not a movement. Movements are governed by the will of the people. Kingdoms are governed by the will of the King."[7] Jesus says, "Blessed is the one who is not offended by me."[8] Do you know why He said that? Because He came to be our King, which means that He came so that His will (and not our will) shall be done, and therein lies the offense. Christ's claim to Kingship stands in opposition to our claim to kingship.

CHRIST'S CLAIM TO KINGSHIP STANDS IN OPPOSITION TO OUR CLAIM TO KINGSHIP.

In Revelation 11:15, John is having a vision. In it, he sees an angel blow a trumpet and proclaim, "The kingdom of the world has become the kingdom of our Lord and of his Christ, and he shall reign forever and ever." Immediately, the people who are surrounding God's throne fall down on their faces and worship God with a hymn. The hymn communicates, "God's reign is beginning and all will be judged; the servants of God will be rewarded and the rebels will be destroyed." It reminds us of a parable that Jesus told in Matthew 13:47–49a: "The kingdom of heaven is like a net thrown into the sea and gathered fish of every kind. When it was full, men drew it ashore and sat down and sorted the good into containers but threw away the bad. So it will be at the end of the age."

It's an unsettling passage from Revelation and a terribly offensive parable from Jesus. This is *no one's* favorite parable! It's offensive because it is clear. Vague teaching is not offensive; clear teaching is. Jesus' meaning and the meaning of Revelation are clear: there are two kinds of people, those who submit to and serve the will of God and those who rebel against it.

C. S. Lewis wrote that, in the end, there are only two kinds of people . . .

> . . . Those who say to God, "Thy will be done," and those to whom God says, in the end, "Thy will be done." All that are in Hell, choose it. Without that self-choice there could be no Hell. No soul that seriously and constantly desires joy will ever miss it. Those who seek find. To those who knock it is opened."[9]

Augustine agrees with Lewis. In his masterful work *The City of God*, he describes two cities: the City of God and the City of Man. These two cities arise from two different and opposed loves. He writes: "Accordingly, two cities have been formed by two loves—the earthly by the love of self, even to the contempt of God; the heavenly by the love of God, even to the contempt of the self."[10]

What you love the most will not only determine the shape of your life, but will also determine the *telos* (purpose) and the future of your life. If you will not yield to God's will in this life, then you will not enjoy His coming kingdom.

The offensive news of the kingdom is that, by nature, we are all inhabitants of the City of Man, the human city. We build our own little kingdoms and we rule over them like miniature kings and queens. This is not only true of us as individuals; it is also true of us as a society. One of the best ways to understand our post-Christian culture of late modernity is "a culture seeking the kingdom without the king."[11] A society seeking the renewal of Jesus without Jesus Himself.

Our culture loudly and proudly seeks social justice, racial healing, economic equality, human dignity for all. However, it does so while not realizing that these kingdom values have been inherited from the Christian faith. And so, our culture seeks this things—these *good* things, these *kingdom* values— but does so while simultaneously rejecting the King.

> **OUR CULTURE SEEKS SOCIAL JUSTICE, RACIAL HEALING, ECONOMIC EQUALITY, HUMAN DIGNITY FOR ALL . . . BUT DOES SO WHILE SIMULTANEOUSLY REJECTING THE KING.**

And then we wonder why we never seem to get there. Why can't we have economic equality? Why can't the racial wounds of our nation be healed? Why can't all humans, men and women, be treated with dignity and value? Because we have rejected the King. We have set our wills against God's will. We work so hard to build the City of Man, all the while expecting it to look like the City of God.

Eclipsing God with the Self

What's more, our own kingdoms obscure our ability to see God's kingdom. Author Flannery O'Connor put it this way:

You are the slim crescent of a moon that I see and my self is the earth's shadow that keeps me from seeing all the moon... what I am afraid of, dear God, is that my self shadow will grow so large that it blocks the whole moon ... I do not know you God because I am in the way.[12]

We can't see the kingdom of God because it is eclipsed by our own little kingdom.

Diagnosing the Eclipse

Now you might be thinking this isn't true for you because you are actively looking for the kingdom of God. You might be thinking, "I am literally eyes-wide-open, looking for God's work in my life, and I can't see it!" Here's what may be happening, friend. You may have your attention so fixed on things going your way, according to your will (your kingdom), that you are unable to see that in the very midst of things *not* going your way, or *against* your will, God is at work, and His kingdom is emerging. One of the best places for me to look for God's kingdom is where things are *not* working out the way I want them to. At least, under those conditions, I can rest assured that the shadow of my own little empire has not eclipsed God's.

So long as my criteria for the kingdom of God is things going my way, then I will probably never have the eyes to see God's will revealed in my life. And so we need a way out. We've seen the comprehensive goodness of the kingdom; both for individuals and for society, but we can't achieve it—it lies outside of our grasp. What's more, our own kingdoms are so in the way that much of the time we can't even see the kingdom of God. What are we to do? How do we surrender our own will to the Lord's will? How do we change our citizenship from the City of Man to the City of God?

PART 3: THE INVITATION OF THE KINGDOM

The answer is found in a garden.

In Matthew 26, on the night between the Last Supper and the crucifixion, we see Jesus praying in the garden of Gethsemane. He knows that He is about to be arrested and beaten and crucified, and He does not want to go through with it. His human will and God's will feel opposed to each other. Jesus has reached the impasse that every single one of us faces: answering the questions, Who is your King? Whose will do you serve?

Have you ever noticed that Jesus prays a modified version of the Lord's Prayer in the garden of Gethsemane? He starts out with "Father," because He knows that He is a child of God and that the Lord is listening to Him with the compassion of a good Father. Then He prays, "If it be possible, let this cup pass from me." This is Jesus' confession of His will: "I don't want to do this." But then, most importantly, He prays, "Nevertheless, not as I will, but as you will." Jesus has chosen His citizenship. He has surrendered His will to God where Adam and Eve and every other human has fought to follow their own will. Jesus faced the fork in the road that leads either to the City of Man or the City of God, and He chose the latter.

In this desperate prayer of Christ, we see the logic behind the order of the Lord's Prayer. First comes "Our Father, who art in heaven, hallowed be thy Name," then comes "thy kingdom come, thy will be done on earth as it is in heaven." The first movement orients us relationally; the second movement orients us directionally because of that relationship.

Subversive Love

Jesus loved all the things He was about to lose. He was about to lose His friends, His family, His job, His comfort, His health, and His life. He loved all those things. They were His will.

But He loved the Father more.

You see, the only way to change what you love is to replace your current love with a stronger love.

Have you ever had someone break up with you? I have. It's the worst. It hurts, and initially it feels like you'll never recover. You had someone you wanted and now they're gone. Your will for your life (and theirs) has been thwarted. How can you learn to live with this? How do you get over your "ex"? Time helps. Having something else to work on helps. But do you know the surefire way to really get over your ex-girlfriend or boyfriend? Meet someone new. Why? Because you cannot *not* love. So don't waste your energy trying not to love the things that you naturally love. It won't work. Rather, you need a new love. As Steve Winwood sang in 1986, "Bring me a higher love!"

But be careful. A higher love, a superior love, will require far more from you than a lesser, inferior love. Consider:

> **Music**: High music requires more of you than low music. A Yo-Yo Ma concert asks more of you than a Macklemore concert. When listening to a cello, you have to concentrate. The music is subtler, nuanced, artful, and therefore requires you to pay attention in a way that Benjamin Hammond Haggerty (Macklemore's

legal name) does not. But the payoff from high music is substantially greater than the payoff from low music.

Food: Elevated gastronomy requires more of you than fast food. Eating a five-course dinner with wine pairings from a master chef and sommelier asks far more of your patience and palate than a Double Down at KFC (a sandwich with two fried chicken breasts in place of the bread). Think I'm a culture snob disguised as a priest? Let's try a different example.

Romance: A spouse requires more of you than a date. Imagine two different couples sitting at two different tables in the same restaurant. The first couple is in their early thirties and on their second date. During the lulls in the conversation they make lingering eye contact, smile, and think about deleting their dating apps because they might have found the one. Now, over on the other side of the restaurant sits a couple in their late forties. They have two children who are home with a babysitter they are paying $12 per hour. They split a salad and pasta dish and pass on dessert. They talk about whether they should fix the broken washing machine or put new tires on the minivan. Then they try to talk about something else because tonight is this month's only date night. Let's say that both couples love each other. Which is the superior love? The kind of affection sparked by a great date has got *nothing* on the kind of covenant love between a couple married fifteen years.

Children: Parenting a child requires more of you than babysitting. I once heard a friend talk about the difference between being a professional nanny and a mother. She had worked as a nanny for a family for years before getting married and having children of her own. She thought that her experience would make the transition to motherhood easy. After all, she had basically done this for years already! Nothing of the sort. Parenting was so much harder.

If these examples are circling in on the truth, then consider what an infinite love might require of you. If a higher love requires more of you than a lesser love, then an infinite love requires *everything* from you.

Jesus has loved you with an infinite love, and the only way to respond to this kind of love is with total surrender—a total surrender of your will to His will.

> IF A HIGHER LOVE REQUIRES MORE OF YOU THAN A LESSER LOVE, THEN AN INFINITE LOVE REQUIRES *EVERYTHING* FROM YOU.

This is why—if your faith is in Jesus and you have received His superior, infinite love—you can actually begin to submit your will to the will of God. Only through the gospel can you truly begin to pray: "Thy kingdom come, thy will be done, on earth as it is in heaven." But we leak. We drift. We get distracted. We forget the gospel.

This is why praying liturgically can help. See, we not only need the gospel to truly pray the Lord's Prayer, we also need the Lord's Prayer to bring us (and our prayers) back to the gospel. Left to my own devices, my prayers drift away from God's will and

God's kingdom toward my will and my own little kingdom. The second movement of the Lord's Prayer draws me out of that self-centered way of praying. When I pray "thy kingdom come, thy will be done on earth as it is in heaven," I am reminded of Christ's infinite love for God the Father and for me. I am reminded of how Jesus surrendered His will to the Father's will and loved me to the end by giving up His own life on the cross for my salvation and for the renewal of all broken things. I am reminded to get out of my own way so that I can see the will of the King revealed in my life and in the world.

GOD IS GOOD. THEREFORE, HE EXISTS

There is wonderfully hopeful news here. When our society decides that God's goodness is a prerequisite for His existence, then the beautiful goodness of Jesus' love in the gospel story proves the existence of the God of the Bible. Of course, this is philosophically illogical, but then again so is most of society in our current cultural moment. I'm not arguing that we *should* think or reason this way, but rather that the majority of our neighbors already do. Therefore, when the church seeks to move out into our secularizing cities with the love of Christ, we meet our neighbors where they are by proclaiming, embodying, and demonstrating the love of God in the gospel first, and then later offer logical reasons for His existence.

In order to do this genuinely our imaginations must be captured by the goodness of God, which is to say, the goodness of His will. When we imagine that God's desires are better, wiser, and preferable to our own desires, we will become the kind of people whose lives declare to the world—God is good.

QUESTIONS FOR DISCUSSION

1. Which realm of the kingdom do you most naturally tend to value? The personal or the common good? What are the consequences of an individual, church, or network of churches becoming unbalanced by choosing one of these over the other?

2. Where have you been able to pray "thy kingdom come, thy will be done," and where have you not? Perhaps you can pray it in your work, but you can't pray it in your relationships. Or maybe you can pray it in your family, but you can't pray it about your money.

3. Where is your own obsession over your own kingdom perhaps obscuring or eclipsing your ability to perceive the kingdom of God coming all around you?

4. How would you describe the difference between your old imagination of the kingdom and the new imagination offered by this stanza of the Lord's Prayer?

PRAYER FOR MEDITATION ALMIGHTY KING, I confess the smallness of my imagination for Your heavenly realm and have allowed my unmet desires to obscure Your work and Your goodness. Quicken my mind and heart to understand Your love poured out in the blood of the cross. Prove to me Your goodness Lord Jesus. Reveal to me, by Your Holy Spirit, the reality of Your coming kingdom as it emerges within us and among us. Amen.

CHAPTER 6

REIMAGINING THE WILDERNESS AS A PLACE OF BOUNTY

Our Father, who art in heaven,
hallowed be thy Name,
thy kingdom come,
thy will be done,
on earth as it is in heaven.
**GIVE US THIS DAY
OUR DAILY BREAD.**
And forgive us our trespasses,
as we forgive those
who trespass against us.
And lead us not into temptation,
but deliver us from evil.
For thine is the kingdom,
and the power, and the glory,
for ever and ever. Amen.

Centuries of secularism have failed to transform eating into something strictly utilitarian. Food is still treated with reverence . . . to eat is still something more than to maintain bodily functions. People may not understand what that "something more" is, but they nonetheless desire to celebrate it. They are still hungry and thirsty for sacramental life.

–ALEXANDER SCHMEMANN

Maybe this is how I die." The thought flashed through my mind as lightning cracked the sky and thunder simultaneously exploded like a concussion bomb. I was on a small boat with six other people out on the Atlantic Ocean with no land in sight when a summer storm rolled in out of nowhere. There was nothing we could do but wait and hope that lightning wouldn't strike the mast (a metal pole conveniently sticking twenty-five vertical feet straight up over the water) and fry us like chicken tenders. I'm not sure which was worse, the fear of dying or the knowledge that I had *no* control over what happened next.

Actually, that's not true. The lack of control was worse. If you're anything like me, you have the courage to face frightening, challenging, difficult situations . . . provided you can face them on your own terms. However, being suddenly and unpreparedly thrown into danger without agency, without any ability to impact the outcome is like suddenly finding yourself free-falling down a dark well with no idea if it is six or sixty or six hundred feet deep. It is unnerving on a whole other level.

DEEPER INTO THE WILDERNESS

The defining feature of the wilderness is that you are not in charge of what happens to you. If it rains, you'll get wet. If the temperature drops, you will be cold. If there isn't a stream nearby, you'll be thirsty. If a grizzly bear attacks, you'll likely die. In the wilderness you are not in charge of what happens to you.

THE WILDERNESS IS WHERE MOST PEOPLE LEARN HOW TO PRAY BECAUSE THE WILDERNESS IS WHERE WE START TO ASK GOD FOR STUFF.

What's more, because you're not in charge, you don't know what's going on and therefore you don't know what to do. This is why the wilderness is paralyzing for people who find themselves lost or stranded in it. We are so accustomed to being (relatively) in control of what happens to us, and we have a good sense of what is happening all around us that we generally know what to do much of the time. But the wilderness strips all of this from us. We lose control, and we don't know what's going on, so we don't know what to do.

Therefore, the wilderness is where most people learn how to pray because the wilderness is where we start to ask God for stuff.

The wilderness is where we get desperate. All the other things aren't working anymore and so we start praying; we start asking God to intervene.

And this brings us to the next section of the Lord's Prayer: "Give us this day our daily bread."

It's a petitionary prayer; it's the kind of prayer that gets us interested in prayer in the first place. Of course, the problem is that we often race through the first two sections of the Lord's Prayer to get to the stuff we really care about. As N. T. Wright puts it: "The danger with the prayer for bread is that we get there too soon."[1] So remember, we pray this only after we've prayed "Our Father in heaven, hallowed be thy Name," and after "thy kingdom come, thy will be done, on earth as it is in heaven."

BREAD

Why did Christ choose bread for His prayer? Why didn't Jesus instruct us to pray, "Give us what we need"? or "Give us our heart's desires"?

Our Lord does not only know what is true, He also knows what is beautiful. He is a poet, *the* poet. Bread is the most elegant, one-word summary of exactly what you and I need. Bread is the bare minimum; bread is summative; bread is symbolic:

Daily bread is the **bare minimum** for survival. If you are stranded on a deserted island and all you have is raw flour and access to fresh water, you can survive. You can't eat the raw flour, but if you mix the flour with water, wait for the naturally occurring yeast to ferment, and start a wood fire, you can make bread and live.

Daily bread is **summative**. The reformer Martin Luther defined daily bread as: "Food, drink, clothes, shoes, houses, farms, fields, lands, money, property, a good marriage, good children, honest and faithful public servants, a just government, favorable weather, health, honors, good friends, loyal neighbors."[2] That just about sums it up!

Daily bread is **symbolic**. Throughout the grand story of Scripture, from Genesis to Revelation, bread symbolizes God's provisional grace to His people.

Consider this example from the book of Exodus. If you've ever read this Old Testament book before, you might remember that Exodus 15 is really exciting. The Israelites are set free from slavery in Egypt. God parts the Red Sea, they walk through, and then, as their enemies pursue them, God brings the waters down and drowns the entire Egyptian army. It's an over-the-top, Michael-Bay-directed, summer blockbuster movie! There are dead enemies, dancing, parties, songs, celebration. For the Israelites, things are looking really good.

And what do they do next? God leads them into the wilderness and that's where things start to go sideways. At the first sign of trouble, they're all ready to turn around, leave God, leave Moses, forget this freedom stuff, and go back to Egypt.

The invitation of Exodus 16 is the invitation to trust God's provision. As the story unfolds, we see that Israel's identity was solidified in the wilderness. The wilderness taught Israel how to be Israel because, in the wilderness, Israel *learned how to depend on God for their daily bread*. In that barren desert, Israel discovered that, with God, the wilderness was actually a place of bounty.

> **IN THAT BARREN DESERT, ISRAEL DISCOVERED THAT, WITH GOD, THE WILDERNESS WAS ACTUALLY A PLACE OF BOUNTY.**

This invitation stands before us today in the Lord's Prayer. "Give us this day our daily bread" invites us to reimagine the wilderness as a place of bounty. It does this in two ways: 1) by exposing our frailty, and 2) by teaching us dependence.

EXPOSING OUR FRAILTY

It is no coincidence that God chose bread (the most basic food staple) as the symbol of His grace when the world was cast into sin through taking and eating the wrong food. When the first humans stretched out their hands for the forbidden fruit, they were demonstrating a desire to exist apart from God, to eat from their own hand and not from His. It is also no coincidence that the first sinful act, which was intended to be a moment of strength and independence, ended up being the very thing that caused humanity to become weak and mortal. In their nakedness, Adam and Eve were exposed as vulnerable. God told Adam that now by the sweat of his face he would eat bread, showing the first people how sin had made them frail.

This frailty persists and keeps popping up over and over again in Scripture. Abraham pretended Sarah was his sister because he was afraid God wouldn't protect them. Jacob dressed up in animal skins to steal his brother's birthright because he was afraid that God wasn't going to take care of him unless he got the inheritance from his dad. Naomi lost her husband and sons and declared that it was exceedingly bitter to her that the Lord's hand had gone out against her (she was in a wilderness of grief and thought God didn't love her anymore).

Think about the Israelites being led into the wilderness. What happens? "The whole congregation of the people of Israel grumbled against Moses and Aaron in the wilderness."[3] The whole congregation, not just a few bad apples—this was everybody! Everybody was complaining, saying, "Would that we had died by the hand of the LORD in the land of Egypt, when we sat by the meat pots and ate bread to the full."[4]

Have you read the first couple chapters of the book of Exodus? Is that what Egypt was like for the Israelites? No! They were enslaved, their children were taken from them and killed. Baby boys were pried from their mothers' arms and cast into the Nile River to drown in front of their parents. That is why Exodus 2:23 tells that "the people of Israel groaned because of their slavery and cried out for help." There weren't a lot of cookouts and baked goods going on in Egypt.

So we see that when the wilderness exposes our frailty the first thing we tend to do is deny it.

Denying Our Frailty

We weren't slaves! We ate well back in Egypt! Full-on denial. A romanticizing of the past. But this is totally normal—not good, but normal. When you start feeling hunger pains, you start wistfully daydreaming about how much food you used to have and how good things used to be. The telltale emotion of denial is **nostalgia**, a romanticized version of the past that either selectively remembers only the good parts or straight up invents a past that never existed. We have to be careful here. Nostalgia denies that the past was just as perilous as the present.

But denying your frailty can get you killed. Some of you may have read the book or seen the movie *Into the Wild*, which tells the story of Christopher McCandless, a young man who hitchhikes to Alaska to live solo in the wilderness. While his adventurous spirit is fun and inspiring, the reader can't help but think his confidence is misplaced. Unsurprisingly, the story ends tragically. Christopher dies of starvation in the Alaskan wilderness because he didn't take his own frailty seriously.

THE TELLTALE EMOTION OF DENIAL IS NOSTALGIA.

What happened next in the desert? God was patient with His grumbling people, and He sent flocks of quail to land near the Israelites in the evening so that they have meat to eat. In the morning, He sent manna. The flakey, white, honey-flavored bread appeared on the ground every morning, six days a week, in an astonishing display of God's provision for His people. He tells them that He will provide all of their food, for free, and they are not to gather extra because He will keep providing it fresh. But what do they do? They don't believe it! They don't listen. Instead, they gather extra manna and keep it overnight, and by morning, Exodus 16:20 says, "it bred worms and stank." So we see that we not only deny our frailty, we also *compensate* for it.

Compensating for Our Frailty

In this scenario, we'll gather enough manna to last many days, just in case God stops providing.

Is there a more perfectly hilarious, and yet spiritually tragic, picture of how we try to compensate for how vulnerable we feel than the empty toilet paper aisles in every grocery store around the United States during the coronavirus pandemic? Americans hoarding dried beans, flour, and paper towels. Pantries and freezers stuffed to overflowing. Bags of kale salad rotting in refrigerators all over the country because, for a hot second, everybody panicked and thought there wasn't going to be enough.

The coronavirus did not make us more vulnerable than we already were, it *revealed* our vulnerability—our frailty—to us. And we immediately started stockpiling.

Telltale Emotion: Anxiety is the telltale emotion of compensating for our frailty. Compensating is trying desperately to bail water out of the boat faster than it's coming in. Compensating is airbrushing your selfies because you feel ugly. Compensating always grows out of anxiety that things are about to implode if you don't do something quick.

Why are there so many anxious Christians? You would think that the subset of society that believes in a sovereign God of love and mercy who has promised to provide for our every need and numbers the hairs on our heads would have little to fret about.

The thing about anxiety, though, is that left unchecked, it will usually morph into anger—and anger requires an object. And that's exactly what we see in this story of Israel. Did you notice how often the word "grumble" is used in this story? It's almost like the author is trying to make a point in Exodus 16:8: "The LORD gives you in the evening meat to eat and in the morning bread to the full, because the LORD has heard your grumbling that you grumble

> **ANXIETY, LEFT UNCHECKED, WILL MORPH INTO ANGER—AND ANGER REQUIRES AN OBJECT.**

against him—what are we? Your grumbling is not against us but against the LORD."

When we feel vulnerable it makes us anxious, and that, in turn, makes us angry. When we're angry, we tend to direct that anger toward other people, especially leaders. The Israelites don't like the fact that God has led them to the wilderness because they feel vulnerable and weak. So they get angry with Moses and Aaron. They're looking for a scapegoat.

Which brings us to the third thing we tend to do when our frailty is exposed. First we deny, then we compensate, and finally, we blame.

Blaming for Our Frailty

If I'm feeling vulnerable, it surely must be someone else's fault. Perhaps it's the politicians, or maybe big businesses, or maybe my parents, or could it be my pastor? We need only go three chapters deep into Holy Scripture before we find people blaming others for their frailty. Adam blames Eve: "This woman you put here with me . . ." Eve blames the serpent: "He tricked me . . ."[5] Do you hear the undertone of bitterness and anger in their blaming?

Telltale Emotion: Anger is the telltale emotion that lets us know we're probably blaming someone for how at-risk we feel. If we feel angry, we likely feel that some grave injustice has been committed against us. (To be clear, injustices do happen and righteous anger is the appropriate emotional response. However, most anger among Christians is less righteous protest and more of the blaming and complaining variety.)

So . . . Nostalgia, Anxiety, Anger—does this sound familiar?

TEACHING US DEPENDENCE

God takes us into the wilderness and gives us these words to pray, "Give us this day our daily bread," and the first reason He does this is to expose our frailty. His intention is to help us become more trusting, content, secure, confident, and dependent people. But in order to do so, He first must help us see that we are not the strong, independent, powerful providers that we think we are!

We have a lot of *unlearning* to do before we can learn to trust God and be dependent on Him as our provider. You and I are not ready to pray "Give us this day our daily bread" until we can admit, even if it's just to ourselves, "I feel vulnerable. I don't feel safe. I don't know if I'll have enough. I don't know if I can make it. I'm afraid. I'm fragile."

The wilderness is God's workshop. It's the place where He will carefully and gently apply pressures until we stop denying, compensating, and blaming.

Approaching God Like a Child

So what does God want from me?

In Matthew 7:7–11, Jesus says:

> "Ask, and it will be given to you; seek and you will find
> ... Which one of you, if his son asks for bread, will give
> him a stone? ... If you then, who are evil, know how to
> give good gifts to your children, how much more will
> your Father who is in heaven give good things to those
> who ask him!"

Jesus is showing us the heart of God the Father. God is saying to us, *I AM YOUR FATHER. Come to Me like a child. Stop denying that you need Me. Stop overcompensating by trying to find a way to get enough money and stuff and networks and resources so that you don't need Me. Stop blaming other people for the fact that you don't trust Me. You are My child, you're My son, you're My daughter—you can come and ask Me. I know you. I know what you need. I'll take care of you.*

Think about it this way: every morning, sometime between 7:00 and 8:00 a.m., our family eats breakfast. My wife and I feed our kids. We have *never* not fed our kids. Sometimes there have been special holiday breakfasts of shrimp and grits with andouille sausage, sautéed peppers, and a tomatillo sauce generously ladled over top. Sometimes there have been whole weeks of plain oatmeal. But there has always been breakfast.

If one of my children crept down the stairs in his pajamas, grabbed four boxes of cereal, and sprinted back up the stairs to his room, I would be concerned. What's going on? If I followed the kid, found him hoarding cereal in his room, asked him what he was doing, and he replied that he was worried there would be no breakfast, that he was just being wise, and that "saving extra cereal for later just makes good sense, Dad," what would I say? Well, it would be funny. But wouldn't it also grieve my heart as a parent? My kid doesn't trust that there will be breakfast tomorrow. This is a problem.

In the gospel of Mark, we find the story of Jesus feeding the five thousand. What's the big idea in this story? Jesus is embodying His heavenly Father's love for His children. He's showing the world that God cares about our hungry bellies. But, you ask, what about when there is *literally* no bread? What about all the people who starve to death? What about all the real need in the world? Are you saying those people didn't pray and ask God to provide?

Jesus addresses that too.

GOD'S WORD IS OUR BREAD

In the beginning of Jesus' ministry, He goes into the wilderness for forty days. He is embodying the story of the people of Israel. And during that time, He fasts. He eats nothing. He is very, very hungry. Hungrier than any of us have ever been. We pick up the story in Matthew 4:3–4: "The tempter came and said to him, 'If you are the Son of God, command these stones to become loaves of bread.'" It's a very reasonable temptation: *Jesus, You're hungry, provide for Yourself; You've got the power to do it.* How does Jesus respond? "Man shall not live by bread alone, but by every word that comes from the mouth of God." Interesting response. Jesus seems to be saying that the most important thing at play here is not wanting to eat bread; the most important thing here is dependence on God the Father. Jesus is saying, *I would rather starve* and die than live on anything *other than bread from God.* Jesus not only perfectly shows us what it looks like to trust God in the wilderness, but He also becomes the *means* by which we can begin to trust God in our wilderness.

GOD'S WORD MADE FLESH IS OUR BREAD

In John 6, we read about an interaction that Jesus had with some religious leaders. They say to Him, essentially, *How do we know that You're legit? When Moses was here, he gave us a sign—manna from heaven—what kind of sign do You give us?* And we might expect Jesus to perform a miracle on the spot—maybe another loaves and fish episode? But instead, Jesus tells them that they've got it all wrong: Moses didn't give them manna, it was a gift from God the Father; and God the Father has given them another gift—the bread of life.

They're intrigued and say, *Okay great, bread of life, we'll take that. Can You get us some?*

And what does Jesus say next? John 6:35 tells us: "I am the bread of life; whoever comes to me shall not hunger, and whoever believes in me shall never thirst."

And how do they respond? More grumbling! We're in Exodus 16 all over again, 1400–1600 or so! Yet, patient Jesus responds beautifully, albeit mysteriously:

> "Truly, I say to you, whoever believes has eternal life. I am the bread of life. Your fathers ate the manna in the wilderness, and they died. This is the bread that comes down from heaven, so that one may eat of it and not die. I am the living bread that came down from heaven. If

anyone eats of this bread, he will live forever. *And the bread that I will give for the life of the world is my flesh.*"[6]

And Jesus did give His flesh. Christ died on the cross so that we can live on the bread of God.

JESUS CHRIST, BREAD OF LIFE

This is why, for nearly two millennia, most Christians in most churches in most places all over the world have sought to regularly come to the Lord's Table to receive the bread (and wine) of Holy Communion. In this simple meal, in a mysterious way that we experience and describe but struggle to precisely define, Jesus is really and truly present with us.

When we go to a worship service and pray the Lord's Prayer, we should be deeply encouraged when, mere minutes after praying "Give us this day our daily bread," the Lord answers our prayer and puts physical bread into our mouths. Bread that is, as Augustine wrote in the fifth century, "the outward and visible sign of an inward and invisible grace."[7]

But Holy Communion is not the answer to the petition "Give us this day our daily bread" because it makes use of *bread*. No, it's deeper than that. It is the answer (or, at least the beginnings of the answer) because the sacrament carries with it the very *presence* of Jesus who is Immanuel, God with us. Remember, our original sin is independence—rejecting God's provision and seeking to provide for ourselves. So when we come to the Lord's Table, we are returning to the way in which we were created to relate to God—dependence on Him.

THE HOLY SPIRIT'S PRESENCE
AS OUR DAILY BREAD

When my kids cry out in the middle of the night (as they often do), what they need is my presence. I can provide all the night-lights, drinks of water, trips to the bathroom, and extra blankets, but what they need first when they wake up and are scared and feel their childlike vulnerability in the dark is the presence of their father. First comes the presence, then comes the provision.

When we petition God for our daily bread, His answer begins with His presence with us in His Holy Spirit who dwells within us. *My child, I am here; there is nothing to fear. Now, tell Me your troubles. Tell Me your needs.* God's presence changes us. If we know that He is with us, then we are transformed.

We become people who need not lapse into nostalgia for an easier, better time when life wasn't so confusing and dangerous. We don't have to deny our own frailty and act like everything would be fine if we could just get back to the way things used to be.

We become people who need not be anxious about the future, wondering if we will have what we need. We don't have to rush around compensating for the day when God will not come through.

We become people who need not be angry about how un-comfortable our lives have become. We don't have to blame *anyone* for how vulnerable we feel.

We can move from denial to acceptance, cheerfully confessing, "I am weak."

We can move from compensation to dependence, humbly confessing, "I need God for everything."

We can move from blame to trust, confidently confessing, "He will provide."

Here's the twist; are you ready? A person who is genuinely able to say, "I am weak, I am totally dependent on God, and I trust Him to provide for me" is, ironically, a *very* strong person. Why? Because this person has surrendered the losing battle of rugged independence and given their allegiance to a King who is far stronger than all enemies.

A PERSON WHO IS GENUINELY ABLE TO SAY, "I AM WEAK, I AM TOTALLY DEPENDENT ON GOD, AND I TRUST HIM TO PROVIDE FOR ME" IS, IRONICALLY, A VERY STRONG PERSON.

This is why the apostle Paul can write in 2 Corinthians 12:9–10:

> But he said to me, "My grace is sufficient for you, for my power is made perfect in weakness." Therefore I will boast all the more gladly of my weaknesses, so that the power of Christ may rest upon me. For the sake of Christ, then, I am content with weaknesses, insults, hardships, persecutions, and calamities. For when I am weak, then I am strong.

The daily bread of God's presence does not eliminate our frailty, rather it *subverts* our frailty by showing us that when we are weak we are strong. Because when we understand our weakness and frailty, we become more dependent on God's presence and provision, which are strong and sure.

Jesus knew that His disciples (perhaps especially Peter) would make every effort, trying their hardest to be the strongest, surest, most confident, most capable spiritual leaders of all time. And He knew they would fail. He knew that they would do their best to plant healthy churches and cultivate thriving communities of vibrant, loving Christian men, women, and children. And He knew that persecution and plague would devastate those churches and communities. He knew that they would follow God to the promised land of the new creation. And He knew that first they would endure a wilderness.

So He gave them this simple prayer: "Give us this day our daily bread." A prayer that would subvert their understanding of what it means to be strong and what it means to have enough. A prayer that would not only teach them about dependence, but would actually make them ever more dependent the more they prayed it. A prayer that would help them become the people they were created and called to be.

REIMAGINING THE WILDERNESS
AS A PLACE OF BOUNTY

In the first episode of season two of the TV show *Alone*, a contestant in the wilderness survival competition makes this dramatic statement about his situation, "It's not this place that has to change, it's me that has to change."[8]

As Christians in Western culture, we succumb to nostalgia for eras of Christendom past, have anxiety about the direction of our culture, and blame it on our increasing vulnerability. It might be time for some of us to begin meditating on that sentence: "It's not this place that has to change, it's me that has to change."

Yes, of course we long for the renewal of all things, the dawning of a bright new day when the kingdom of God fully and finally arrives and all is at last restored and put right. The promised land is real, and we are right to anticipate it. But until then, we must journey through the wilderness; and what kind of wilderness is this? Is it a barren wasteland of emptiness? Or is it a place of provision ... even bounty?

The surprising fruit on the other side of the subversive prayer, "Give us this day our daily bread," is that we begin to see bread everywhere. Our eyes are opened to see the manna that covers the ground like dew. If God is truly present with us (and He is), then there is always enough.

We may feast on His Word every day.

We may feast at His Table every week.

We may know the consolation of His presence every moment.

The defining feature of the wilderness is that you are not in charge of what happens to you. That is still true, but you may ask for daily bread—and there is a God who hears and provides.

QUESTIONS FOR DISCUSSION

1. What aspects of your life feel most wilderness-like and out of your control?

2. In what ways has your own frailty been exposed in this season of life? What has that been like for you?

3. In what area of life are you most resistant to (and therefore, most in need of) learning dependence on God?

4. How is your imagination changing and expanding to see God's bountiful provision in your wilderness?

PRAYER FOR MEDITATION

GRACIOUS LORD, make me to know my frailty and weakness. Reveal to me my utter dependence on You. Teach me to feed upon Your Word. Nourish me, by the broken body and shed blood of Jesus, at Your banquet table. Fill me with Your Spirit's presence. All that I may receive daily bread from Your hand. Amen.

CHAPTER 7

REIMAGINING LIFE AS FREE

Forgiveness is the name of love practiced among people who love poorly. The hard truth is that all people love poorly. We need to forgive and be forgiven every day, every hour increasingly. That is the great work of love among the fellowship of the weak that is the human family.

–HENRI NOUWEN

Our Father, who art in heaven,
  hallowed be thy Name,
  thy kingdom come,
  thy will be done,
    on earth as it is in heaven.
Give us this day our daily bread.
And **FORGIVE US OUR TRESPASSES,
  AS WE FORGIVE THOSE
    WHO TRESPASS AGAINST US**.
And lead us not into temptation,
  but deliver us from evil.
For thine is the kingdom,
  and the power, and the glory,
  for ever and ever. Amen.

In 1993, teenager Oshea Israel was arrested, tried, and sentenced to twenty-five years in prison for shooting and killing twenty-year-old Laramiun Byrd at a party.[1]

At the trial, Laramiun's mother, Mary Johnson, sat in the courtroom looking at her son's murderer. Mary was and is a Christian. And she thought about this phrase in the Lord's Prayer: forgive us our debts as we forgive our debtors. She knew that her Christian faith compelled her to forgive Oshea. So, she stood up and forced the words out, "I forgive you." But as she later reported, she said the words, but she did not feel them or mean them. She was still consumed with anger, hatred, resentment, and bitterness.

As a follower of Jesus, she believed forgiveness was the right thing to do, but as a human being she found herself unable to do it. How do you forgive someone who has taken your child from you? How do you forgive someone who has hurt you this deeply? At that moment, forgiveness did not feel like the right thing to do, or the good thing to do, and it certainly did not feel *possible*—even if she had wanted to.

THE WALKING WOUNDED

It's a dramatic story, but no doubt you can empathize with this struggle. Nearly all of us have people who have truly wounded us. We are all walking around with scars on our minds and hearts and maybe even on our bodies from the sins of other people. Our scars are the consequences of other people's sin. We're not talking about misunderstandings or disagreements or differences of opinion, but real, intentional hurt. Sometimes forgiveness doesn't feel possible or even desirable. How *do I do this?* Why *would I even want to do this?*

To make matters even more complicated, nearly all of us, in layers deep underneath the skin, have a nagging sense of guilt. Perhaps you might have thought that you were the only one who struggled with this. Good news and bad news: you are not alone. If you search online for the phrase "get rid of guilt," here are just a few hits that pop up:

- Five ways to get rid of guilt and move on with your life
- Nine ways to talk yourself out of unnecessary guilt
- How to eliminate the guilt that is slowly draining away your life
- Five science-backed tips for getting rid of guilt
- How to get rid of guilt instantly

The Christian belief from the teaching of the Bible is that guilt is not primarily a psychological issue to be alleviated, but rather a relational consequence of sin. Our sin is a rebellion that wounds the heart of God and estranges us from Him—this is the source of our guilt. And so, the Bible teaches that the solution to guilt is not therapy but forgiveness.

The consequences of other people's sin hurt the world, and they hurt us. What's more, the consequences of our own sin not only mess up our lives but leave us mired in guilt. We need a way out from the consequences of our sin and from the collective sins of the world.

Here, this fourth stanza of the Lord's Prayer not only reminds us of the importance of forgiveness, but (if we seek to understand gospel forgiveness) then we find that forgiveness subverts the consequences of sin. What do I mean? Let's consider it from three angles: the appeal, the cost, and the wonder of forgiveness.

The Appeal of Forgiveness

In the book of Leviticus, chapter 25, God gives the people of Israel a series of laws and commands that are to govern their society once they reach the promised land. Remember, they are wandering in the wilderness for forty years, and they are headed toward this promised land. God is getting them ready for it by telling them ahead of time what kind of shape life will take once they are there.

God gives them a fascinating law called the Year of Jubilee. Here's the basic premise: after forty-nine years, on the tenth day of the seventh month (on a special day called the Day of Atonement), a trumpet would sound and a grand announcement would be made. The announcement was for everyone to return to their original property, the farmland of their parents and grandparents. The idea was, every fifty years, all debts were forgiven, nobody planted any new crops, everyone took a big break from work, and all people were restored to whatever land they lost in poor business decisions or droughts or floods. It's a reset button for the entire economy and a call to celebration.

Why did God command this? Two reasons: a practical limit and a spiritual reminder. There's a practical limit being established here. Just imagine what this kind of practice would do for society. This is a safeguard against generational poverty. It allows for people to work hard, get ahead, acquire more land, plant and harvest crops, and make a profit; but it keeps the rich from getting richer, and richer, and richer and acquiring more, and more, and more land, while the poor get poorer and poorer and have fewer and fewer resources to leverage. At a very practical level, this safeguards the middle class; it provides for a healthier society where everybody has enough to live.

Not only does this law set a practical limit, it serves as a spiritual reminder. In Leviticus 25:23, God says, "The land is mine. For you are strangers and sojourners with me."

God is reminding His people that this promised land is an undeserved gift. God has rescued them from slavery in Egypt, led them through the wilderness, and given them this rich and abundant place as their home. They are to live in perpetual gratitude for God's mercy, and one of the best reminders of that is to require that they show mercy to others. Summarized in one sentence: God has dealt graciously with you, now you deal gracefully with each other.

The Year of Jubilee gives us a vision for what culture and society can look like when they are founded upon grace and forgiveness as opposed to fairness and natural consequences. A society founded upon what is natural and fair is a brutal place to live. If your crop gets ruined, your family will starve. If you mismanage your land, not only will a wealthier farmer come and buy you out; but your children and their children will, for generations, be doomed to servitude. This has been true of every society since Genesis 3, ever since humanity fell into sin. The debt forgiveness of Jubilee partially subverts the consequences of society marred by sin.

If we phrased it in catechetical form, we would say:

Q: How can a society of sinful people thrive?
A: *When grace and forgiveness are the foundations and not fairness and natural consequences.*

At first blush, this sounds very appealing.

So many people today are in debt. You may have student loans you're struggling to pay off. You may have a mortgage that costs you more than you can afford every month. You may have credit card debt that follows you everywhere you go. You may have financial problems so embarrassingly enormous that you keep them a secret from everyone, even your closest friends. So a Year of Jubilee sounds *great*! A society founded on forgiveness sounds appealing to everyone except the very wealthy.

But wait, this appeal is a bit too quick and too easy. We have not yet considered the cost of forgiveness.

The Cost of Forgiveness

In Matthew 18:21, Peter comes to Jesus and asks a question that he thinks is going to win him some points. It's like that moment in class when the super annoying student raises their hand and asks a question that isn't really a question but rather a statement that just shows off the fact that they did the reading. Peter asks, "How many times do I have to forgive someone? As many as seven times?" Standard Jewish rabbinical teaching in the first century commanded three times. Three strikes and you're out if you're a first-century Jew. So, Peter thinks he's going above and beyond. *Hey, Jesus, check me out. How about seven times?*

Jesus, not impressed, says, *How about seventy-seven times?* (Which is first-century Jewish slang for an infinite number of times.) Then Jesus tells a story to back it up with the parable of the unforgiving servant. In this story, a servant has a massive debt forgiven by the king but is unwilling to forgive a tiny debt owed to him by a fellow servant. The man owes a government-bailout-four-trillion-dollar-sized debt, but he can't forgive someone who owes him lunch money.

Jesus tells this parable to illustrate what our debt to God is like compared to other people's debts to us. Put it another way: the parable shows us the staggering gravity of our sin and offense against God compared to the relatively small offenses that other people inflict on us.

You see, the Year of Jubilee is appealing, but that is because we think we fundamentally *deserve* forgiveness. We think it's unjust that we would be in debt. We say we want forgiveness, but what we actually mean is fairness.

I want the fairness because I don't see myself as the first servant, needing to be forgiven a massive debt . . . because I don't think of my sin as primarily against God. When I think of the wrongs I commit, I tend to think almost exclusively in terms of my relationships to other people.

❁ ❁ ❁ ❁

Last night, during the manic evening bedtime routine hour, I lost my temper and raised my voice at my kids. After the last pajama-ed monkey was tucked in bed and I was finally downstairs, the guilt set in. I trudged back upstairs and went from room to room apologizing to each child for being a grump and reassuring them of my love. Fifteen minutes later, I was back downstairs cleaning up the kitchen when I realized I hadn't finished apologizing. So, I went to the laundry room where my long-suffering wife was tirelessly folding an Everest-sized mountain of clothes and apologized to her for yelling at the kids. They are her kids too. When I sin against them, I sin against her. Twenty minutes later, after the kitchen was finally cleaned up, I realized I was still not done apologizing. I had not yet repented to the Lord.

Now, at this moment, you might be tempted to roll your eyes and think that this is a classic case of over-spiritualizing. *Would you lighten up, man? That's a lot of apologizing for a relatively small thing that nearly every parent on the planet does every day. Don't I just need the words of John Candy from* Home Alone: *"Kids are resilient"?*[2]

No need to over-spiritualize, let's just name some true things:

- My children are miraculous creatures that, just a few years ago, *did not exist*. And then, through the absolutely astonishing miracle of conception and birth, they developed into living, breathing, talking, laughing, goofing-off children.
- These children bear the image of the triune God and are therefore imbued with divine dignity and eternal worth.
- I, the dad, did not create the children. I do not sustain their lives. I did not give them any of their remarkable gifts or abilities.
- As I age, I will one day be dependent on these children not only for my own well-being, but also for the future continuance of the human race.
- God has entrusted these unique, divine image bearers to my care for a short season. As a parent, I have been directly commissioned by God to raise these four children. I have orders from on high, a sacred duty to perform.

And I yelled at *all* of them because *one* of them accidentally smeared blue sparkle toothpaste on his pajamas.

Yep. I deserve to be damned.

Asking forgiveness from my kids and wife is essential, but secondary. My wrongs against them are first and foremost wrongs committed against their creator, provider, guardian, redeemer, and Lord.

But let's be honest, shall we? I don't want to repent at that deep level most days, and I bet you don't either. So, here's how I buffer myself: I measure myself against the worst people I know. Throw in the internet and the 24-hour catastrophe/scandal/ crisis news cycle where we are hyper-exposed to all of the worst things people are doing all over the world, and you and I naturally develop feelings of moral superiority. Sure, we're not perfect. But what are our little imperfections compared to the atrocities that are being committed by monstrous bigots, racists, misogynists, and terrorists? Sure, we say, I'm no saint, but I don't take my shoes off on airplanes. I'm *nothing* like *those* people.

In the wake of the #MeToo movement, Claire Dederer wrote an article in *The Paris Review* titled, "What Do We Do with the Art of Monstrous Men?" The first half of her article is what you might expect. She is asking whether we should boycott the work of people who do terrible things. But then, she makes a brilliant insight, "When you're having a moral feeling, self-congratulation is never far behind."[3] In other words, when we voice moral outrage, part of that is good and right; it is appropriate to condemn corrupt behavior. But part of that condemnation can also be a form of self-congratulation. We're implying that *we* would *never* do such a thing. We are better than that.

Why would we feel the need to congratulate ourselves? Dederer writes:

> I can sense there's something entirely unacceptable lurking inside me. Even in the midst of my righteous indignation... I know that, on some level, I'm not an entirely upstanding citizen myself.... In everyday deed and thought, I'm a decent-enough human. But I'm something else as well, something vaguely resembling a,

well, monster . . . I suppose this is the human condition, this sneaking suspicion of our own badness."[4]

This is why people like you and me can find the forgiveness of the Year of Jubilee appealing and yet still struggle to forgive other people. We believe we deserve to be forgiven more than others. We have a deep inner belief in our own moral superiority. This is why it is absolutely necessary for every single person to come to face-to-face with the crucifixion of Jesus. The death of Jesus shows us, in bloody, visceral terms, what forgiveness costs God.

THE FORGIVENESS THAT GOD OFFERS IS FREE FOR US, BUT IT IS NOT FREE FOR HIM.

The forgiveness that God offers is free for us, but it is not free for Him. Our sinful rebellion against God is so enormous, so cataclysmically destructive to the fabric of the universe, that it required the death of God to heal the wound. And so, when you contemplate a God that you have so deeply offended and wounded that the death penalty was necessary, and then to think that the same God you offended accepted the death penalty in your place, you should be overcome simultaneously both with enormous weight of your own sin and yet the even greater strength of the love of God for you. If you can see your own sin and God's love at the same time, it'll knock you off your feet.

This is why, for a Christian, the cross of Jesus is both: humiliating and heartening, convicting and comforting.

To shame our sins He blushed in blood;
He closed His eyes to show us God;
Let all the world fall down and know
That none but God such love can show.[5]

- Bernard of Clairvaux

Under the shadow of the cross, we are forgiven, and so that is the place where we turn and begin to forgive others. Under the cross we realize that we are the first servant who has had an enormous, unpayable debt forgiven, and so the offenses of others, even the monstrous crimes of others, begin to look a little smaller. Under the cross, we realize that we are the Israelites who have been set free from Egypt, guided through the wilderness, and given a promised land—and so we can participate in a Year of Jubilee and forgive the debts of others.

I love the way Bono (lead singer of U2) describes how God's grace turns our spiritual assumptions about the world upside down:

> You see, at the center of all religions is the idea of Karma. You know, what you put out comes back to you: an eye for an eye, a tooth for a tooth, or in physics—in physical laws—every action is met by an equal or an opposite one. It's clear to me that Karma is at the very heart of the universe. I'm absolutely sure of it. And yet, along comes this idea called Grace to upend all that "as you reap, so you will sow" stuff. Grace defies reason and logic. Love interrupts, if you like, the consequences of your actions...[6]

His point is this: God's love for us, expressed in His forgiveness, subverts the consequences of our sin.

Forgiveness means that we do not reap what we sow.

Forgiveness means we do not get what we deserve.

Forgiveness means that what goes around does not come around.

Forgiveness means that, for a Christian, the world is not a place of fairness and natural consequence.

This frees up our imaginations to begin dreaming with God about His kingdom and how we can begin to participate in the here and now.

The Wonder of Forgiveness

The story of Mary Johnson finding herself unable to forgive Oshea Israel, her son's murderer, has a surprising ending that no would have imagined. Twelve years later, Mary went to visit Oshea in prison.

> "I don't know you and you don't know me," Johnson recalls saying. "You didn't know my son and he didn't know you, so we need to lay down a foundation and get to know one another."[7]

The conversation that ensued proved cathartic for both Israel and Johnson. They talked about Johnson's son. Israel acknowledged what he had done, and asked through tears for Johnson's forgiveness. He also asked her for a hug.

When the meeting concluded, and Israel had returned to his cell, Johnson reflected in awe about what had just happened. "I just hugged the man that murdered my son," she said to herself.

"And I instantly knew that all anger and animosity, all the stuff I had in my heart for 12 years … was over."[8]

Fast forward. Israel was released from prison in 2010 and has become very close to the mother of the man he killed. Johnson describes Israel as her "spiritual son" and looks forward to seeing him graduate from college and potentially get married—two things she never got to see her biological son do.

When Mary Johnson got married, Israel walked her down the aisle.

But the closeness between Johnson and Israel is more than just emotional and spiritual—it's also geographical. With Johnson's approval, Israel moved into the apartment immediately adjacent to hers. They are now neighbors, dwelling together in peace.

And you might think to yourself, *Wow, that must have required so much strength to forgive like that, to forgive and adopt the person who killed your son.*

No! It did not require strength. That's exactly the problem that Mary Johnson hit the first time around. She tried in the courtroom to muster up the strength to forgive, and she couldn't do it. It is the gospel that makes this kind of forgiveness possible because the gospel is, quite literally, the story of a Father who forgives and adopts the people who killed His son.

REIMAGINING THE WORLD

And so, if the sheer wonder of the gospel is animating our imaginations, we will become people who receive forgiveness and go out into the world heralding the Year of Jubilee by forgiving others. We will be people who don't live by the rules of fairness and natural consequences; we will be people who are constantly subverting the empire of "get what you deserve" by forgiving, and therefore, with grace, receiving and giving what is not deserved.

Let's speak plainly about receiving forgiveness and forgiving others. They are both an event and process.

How to Receive Forgiveness

This begins as an event. There must be a moment when you drop to your knees and truly confess your sins, telling the truth about yourself to God and asking for Him to forgive.

This is the moment when we start to deal with our guilt.

This kind of confession has absolutely no sense of entitlement. You are asking for an unpayable debt to be forgiven.

You may be new to exploring the church and the Christian faith and you've never done this before. If so, you are invited to confess for the very first time, to truly surrender yourself to God, trusting that He will not condemn you, but will forgive you.

Or perhaps you believe, but you've never really done it yourself. You believe you're sinful (maybe with a lowercase "s"), but you don't think of yourself as having an unpayable debt to God. You don't think of yourself as culpable in regard to the cross of Jesus. And so even though you've been in church for years, maybe even decades, you are also invited to truly confess for the very first time. Admit that all your efforts at being a good Christian don't credit you anything with God and that you *need* the blood of the crucified Jesus to be forgiven a debt that you will never be able to pay on your own. This the only way to begin to deal with guilt.

Or maybe you have truly confessed before. Maybe confession

is a frequent and regular part of your daily and weekly habit, but perhaps you struggle to *believe* that you're forgiven. The good news for you is that receiving God's forgiveness is not only an event, but also a process.

There is an ongoing process to believing that you are forgiven. As Robert Farrar Capon writes, "Grace cannot prevail until our lifelong certainty that someone is keeping score has run out of steam."[9]

If you have received the forgiveness of God the Father through the blood of Jesus and have been united to Christ in baptism, then friend, God is not keeping score with you. There is no running tally of bad things you've done.

Remember 1 Corinthians 13? Love keeps no record of wrongs. There is no scoreboard, no list, no secret file. God truly loves you. He is not keeping a record of the wrong things you've done. It may take a while for the feeling of being forgiven to sink it, but it will eventually.

Receiving forgiveness is both an event and a process.

How to Forgive Others

Again, this is both an event and a process.

Forgiving those who have hurt you begins as an event. There is a moment where, standing in the shadow of the cross, in full knowledge of all that God has done to forgive you, your heart shifts and you see your enemy, the person who has wronged you, as a prodigal child who is also loved and forgiven

> YOU SEE YOUR ENEMY, THE PERSON WHO HAS WRONGED YOU, AS A PRODIGAL CHILD . . . AND YOUR HEART GOES OUT TO THEM.

by God. And your heart goes out to them. Wonder of wonders, you begin to feel compassion for the person who has hurt you!

This is only possible through the gospel. Jesus hangs upon the cross and begs God the Father to forgive His executioners. The Spirit of the same Jesus dwells within you and gives you the capacity for that kind of compassion.

Forgiving others is an event. But, as those of you who are a bit older already know, it is also a process. You will keep practicing forgiveness for the people who have hurt you. You will have to return to that place of forgiveness over and over and over again before it really sinks in and becomes permanent in your own heart.

One practical thing you can do to help the process is refusing to keep records of other people's wrongs. All of us, from early childhood, develop the nasty habit of remembering all the wrong things other people do, and it is deliciously easy to scroll through the list of hurts that others have inflicted.

That's why you have got to burn the list. When you burn that mental list of hurts, you are surrendering your ability to dangle those hurts over people; you're surrendering the evidence of your better-ness and your moral superiority. Burning those lists will probably feel a little bit like death—a kind of death to self, crucifixion even of the arrogant self who thinks you deserve forgiveness but someone else doesn't.

REIMAGINING LIFE AS FREE

Forgiveness has a certain appeal, doesn't it? We are drawn to the concept of a Year of Jubilee and the vision of a culture and society founded upon grace and forgiveness. But we check ourselves because the cost of forgiveness is higher than we initially imagine. We don't tend to think of our sins as being primarily against God and so we don't see ourselves as the first servant in Jesus' parable, the one who owes the unpayable debt. Then we remember that, in the crucifixion of Jesus, the unpayable debt is paid on our behalf, and the gospel is the story of a God who loves us to the point of death.

This sparks wonder in our minds and hearts where the love of Christ ignites our imaginations to see ourselves, others, and the world differently—through the lens of freedom. No longer is this a place of fairness and consequence, but a world of grace and forgiveness. Light and free, we move through this new world as heralds of the true Year of Jubilee, which is to say, heralds of the kingdom of God. We announce to our families, friends, neighbors, and coworkers that, in Jesus, forgiveness has the final world and in Him all debts are canceled. We prove that this new kingdom reality is more than mere ideas and words when we extend radical forgiveness to others who have inflicted very real hurts against us.

And so we pray, "Forgive us our trespasses, as we forgive those who trespass against us."

QUESTIONS FOR DISCUSSION

1. Who has inexcusably wronged you? Why should they have known better?
2. Who have you inexcusably wronged? Why should you have known better?

3. Where in your life does the event of receiving the forgiveness of God still need to occur? How are you still in the process of receiving God's forgiveness?

4. Where in your life does the event of giving forgiveness to someone still need to occur? How are you still in the process of giving forgiveness to someone that has hurt you?

5. How would you describe the difference between your old imagination of forgiveness and the new imagination offered by this stanza of the Lord's Prayer?

PRAYERS FOR MEDITATION

Three Sample Beginnings to a Prayer for Forgiveness:

BLESS ME, for I have sinned . . .

JESUS, Son of David, have mercy on me . . .

LORD JESUS, I wish to tell the truth . . .

CHAPTER 8

REIMAGINING OURSELVES AS SAFE

Oh make the devil leave me alone
Oh make the devil leave me alone
Oh Lord the devil's on my back,
   trying to get me back
Oh make the devil leave me alone!
**–MARY JAMES, PRISONER AT
THE STATE PENITENTIARY IN
PARCHMAN, MISSISSIPPI, 1939**

And there was war in heaven.
–REVELATION 12:7 NASB

Our Father, who art in heaven,
   hallowed be thy Name,
   thy kingdom come,
   thy will be done,
      on earth as it is in heaven.
Give us this day our daily bread.
And forgive us our trespasses,
   as we forgive those
      who trespass against us.
And **LEAD US NOT INTO
   TEMPTATION,
   BUT DELIVER US FROM EVIL.**
For thine is the kingdom,
   and the power, and the glory,
   for ever and ever. Amen.

This is, in my opinion, the most difficult phrase to understand in the Lord's Prayer. For two reasons:

1. It doesn't mean what it sounds like it means.
2. It takes us into deep, complex, and uncomfortable spiritual waters.

This stanza of the prayer sounds like it means something like, *God, please don't tempt me to sin and protect me from dangerous, harmful things.* Why doesn't it mean that? Scripture regularly describes God not as tempting people to sin or maliciously hurting them, but rather as testing people by bringing them into difficult situations where they experience suffering and must choose between obedience or disobedience. The God of the Bible is not a tempter, but a tester. "Let no one say when he is tempted, 'I am being tempted by God,' for God cannot be tempted with evil, and he himself tempts no one."[1] The God of the Bible does not promise to protect us from suffering, but rather to use suffering to help us grow and to accomplish His good purposes: "And we know that for those who love God all things work together for good, for those called according to his purpose."[2] So, if you have ever thought about this line in the Lord's Prayer as basically a prayer against temptation and suffering, then fear not, you are normal. Unfortunately, you're also wrong. As theologian Karl Barth cautions:

> We are wrong when we cry, deliver us from any possible danger or cause for sorrow. In this petition of the Lord's Prayer we are not concerned with evils of this sort, with these minor temptations, which are of a relative and bearable nature.[3]

If that's not what this line means, then what does it mean? To answer this question, we are going to have to go deep into the nature of evil, which, of course, nobody wants to do. But we must do it if we are to better understand our world, our lives, our God, and the invitation to put our faith in the gospel.

We're going to have to talk about evil.

CONFUSION OVER GOOD & EVIL

Now, the problem of evil in the world is something we all feel and experience, even though we live in a society without a shared morality. While we do not all agree on *what* is generally right and wrong, nearly all of us recognize the existence of evil.

Imagine you're touring some historical landmarks in Europe. You take a tour of an ancient cathedral and some folks on the tour want to sit in quiet awe and some want to chat irreverently. Why? Because some people find that the sanctuary draws their hearts toward a transcendent reality and some scoff at such ideas. But then the same group of people take a tour of former Nazi concentration camp at Auschwitz, and *everyone* is silent. Why? There is a shared experience that the place is evil.

An encounter with evil makes us hunger for an ordered, moral universe. We want moral order because we desperately want to interpret our life experiences, especially our experiences of suffering, as meaningful. We need to know that our pain means something. We need to know that our hardships are not simply the result of cold, indifferent chance. Andrew Delbanco, a professor at Columbia University (and to my knowledge, not a professing Christian), writes: "A gulf has opened up in our culture between the visibility of evil and the intellectual resources available for coping with it."[4] In other words, our world is just as evil as it ever was; however, most people do not have a guiding narrative, sufficient language, or mental framework for understanding and responding to evil.

So, we've got some work to do. In order for us to pray "lead us not into temptation, but deliver us from evil," we must first understand the story of evil; second, perceive the threat of evil; and third, hope in the redemption from evil.

UNDERSTANDING THE STORY OF EVIL

Islam teaches that evil is divine retribution for sins committed in this life. Hinduism teaches that evil is punishment for sins from past lives. Now, what other stories do people believe about evil?

- There is no evil aside from human evil.
- Human evil almost always has a rational explanation (e.g., poor upbringing, abuse, lack of education).
- People who believe in demons are uneducated, backward fools.
- Belief in personified evil (i.e., Satan) is the equivalent of believing that Sauron, Darth Vader, or Voldemort are real.

Now, what about most Christians? Even people who identify as Christians rarely think, talk, or act as if Satan and demons are real. This either comes from a place of not wanting to appear crazy or weird or from a place of fear and thinking their belief may actually attract demonic attention. This kind of person tends to think of Satan as *he-who-must-not-be-named.*

But then there is a whole other kind of person, the kind who is overly interested in the supernatural. The past few decades have seen a rise in popularity of Wicca, interest in occult practices, and the softer-more-gentle-seeming approach that sees the world through the lens of spiritual energy. Online businesses that sell crystals supposedly infused with positive spiritual energy are booming. Additionally, there are many Christians for whom everything is interpreted through the lens of spiritual warfare. In some circles, there is an obsession with angels and demons, complete with special prayers and incantations to protect oneself against supernatural evil.

Though it may surprise you, everything we've just mentioned actually has little to do with the biblical story of evil. Not only is the biblical story different, it's also far more complex and nuanced. Throughout the story of the Bible, we see that evil is both personal and systemic, natural and supernatural, opposed to God and subject to God. If the church in our time can recapture the comprehensive, holistic truth of this story, we will be far better prepared, not only to cope with the evils of our age, but also to help and comfort our unbelieving neighbors who are troubled and wounded by wickedness.

Evil Is Both Personal & Systemic

According to the Bible, evil is personal. The story of Scripture frequently describes evil spiritual beings that afflict humans. The serpent deceives Eve in Genesis 3; Satan attacks a man's property, family, and health in Job 1; the prince of the kingdom of Persia (a dark spirit) opposes God's angelic messenger in Daniel 10; and a demon torments a man in Luke 8 and possesses a girl in Acts 16. On a more familiar note, evil is also inflicted by individual humans. Jesus teaches that we are not only victims of evil, but that evil actually comes from inside of us.[5]

But evil is also systemic. Consider the words of the prophet Isaiah:

> The way of peace they do not know, and there is no
> justice in their paths; they have made their roads

crooked; no one who treads on them knows peace. Therefore, justice is far from us, and righteousness does not overtake us; we hope for light, and behold, darkness, and for brightness, but we walk in gloom.[6]

The prophet is describing a world where there is not only personal evil in the form of demons and individual human sin, but where there is also systemic evil: injustice, oppression, and systems that are bent, crooked.

On a lighter note, you've probably encountered this dynamic when you've visited the DMV. You may have had a particularly unhelpful person *and* you've also probably thought, "This whole system doesn't work." On a much more serious note, many people of color in the United States can testify to the corrosive, debilitating effects of systemic racism against people with black and brown skin. As the Rev. Dr. Esau McCauley wrote in a *New York Times* article: "People can rob you at gunpoint and governments can rob you through eminent domain. Both are wrong."[7] The story of the Bible makes sense of our experiences by telling the story of evil that is both personal and systemic.

Evil Is Both Natural & Supernatural

By "natural," we simply mean something that occurs in the physical world that we can observe with our five senses. This includes disaster, disease, and evil deeds done by humans. All of us are probably most aware of natural evils perpetrated by people, so let's now consider depersonalized, natural evils, as described in Ecclesiastes 9:12: "Like fish that are taken in an evil net, and like birds that are caught in a snare, so the children of man are snared at an evil time, when it suddenly falls upon them." If we are to take the words of King Solomon seriously, then we must conclude that the Indian Ocean tsunami of 2004 that killed over 225,000 people was not an innocent wave. The coronavirus pandemic that killed millions worldwide is not an innocent virus. Natural evil exists, and it is important for us to identify it as such. Otherwise, how are we to make sense of our pain when children die of cancer or when Hurricane Katrina floods the Lower Ninth Ward in New Orleans? These are evils resulting from the fall into sin, which corrupted every molecule in the material world.

Evil is also supernatural, meaning there exists a kind of evil that cannot be sensed in the physical realm. Evil, according to Scripture, includes things like demonic temptation, possession, and oppression.[8] Evil can also exist in human thoughts. Evil is not limited to the physical world or to spiritual beings; it can dwell in the mind and desire of any person.[9] So evil is both personal and systemic, and evil is both natural and supernatural.

Evil Is Both Opposed to God & Subject to God

Evil is defined as that which is opposed to God. In Genesis 3, the serpent enters the garden of Eden already opposing God and humanity. In John 8:44, Jesus says, "The devil . . . was a murderer from the beginning, and does not stand for truth, because there is no truth in him. When he lies, he speaks out of his own character, for he is a liar and the father of lies." We are to understand that evil is not defined fundamentally as "things we don't like," but rather as anything that is opposed to God. God is the stable reality that evil rails against. God is truth; thus, lying is evil. God is love; thus, hate is evil. God is the source of life; thus, death is evil.

But we make a mistake if we think that evil is somehow the

bad genie that got out of the bottle and is on the loose. Evil has never, for a second, escaped from outside of God's control, which is to say, God's sovereignty. We see this most clearly in the miracles of Jesus. The miracles of Jesus demonstrate God's power over evil in all its forms. When Jesus casts out demons, He demonstrates power over personalized, supernatural evil. When Jesus feeds the hungry, He demonstrates power over the systemic evils of poverty and emptiness. When Jesus heals the sick, He demonstrates power over the evils of biological disease and physical injury. When Jesus calms the storm, He demonstrates His power over the evil of natural disasters. The miracles of Jesus are not publicity stunts, they are meant as signposts that point not only to God's opposition of evil, but to His sovereignty over it. The author of 1 John comforts the church with these words: "Little children, you are from God and have overcome them, for he who is in you is greater than he who is in the world."[10]

> **THE MIRACLES OF JESUS ARE . . . MEANT AS SIGNPOSTS THAT POINT NOT ONLY TO GOD'S OPPOSITION OF EVIL, BUT TO HIS SOVEREIGNTY OVER IT.**

DIAGNOSING THE DANGER

Now, you might be thinking that this has been a nice little academic, theological exercise in which we have categorized, labeled, and safely filed away various forms of evil. Let's live a little more dangerously and turn the lens on ourselves, shall we? There is a real and present danger here for all of us with two potentially fatal consequences. The danger lies in having a far too narrow view of evil. People tend to see *some* forms of evil and are blind to others. They take some forms of evil seriously and dismiss others. The twin consequences of this are:

1. You are most likely to participate in the form of evil that you dismiss.
2. You are most vulnerable to harm from the forms of evil that you don't take seriously.

For example, if you take the personal nature of evil seriously, you may be faithful in praying against demonic evil in your life and in the world; but you may be completely unaware that you are oppressed by and even participate in forms of systemic evil in our culture and society (e.g., people who owned slaves in my city of Richmond, Virginia, prayed against the devil). In the same ways, you may be faithful in working against natural evils like the coronavirus; but you might dismiss the idea that a person can be oppressed by a demon in a way that clouds and darkens their thoughts, feelings, emotions, beliefs, and even their actions. This leaves you dangerously vulnerable. Or perhaps you take both personal and systemic and natural and supernatural evil seriously, but you tend to think of it like the dark side of the "Force" in Star Wars (equal and opposite from the light side), which leaves you anxious and fearful because you are forgetting or simply underestimating the sovereignty of God. Biblically speaking, Satan is not equal and opposite to God. Satan is a *created* being. If he has an opposite, it would be Michael the Archangel, not God.

> **YOU ARE MOST LIKELY TO PARTICIPATE IN THE FORMS OF EVIL YOU DISMISS, AND YOU ARE MOST VULNERABLE TO HARM FROM FORMS OF EVIL YOU DON'T TAKE SERIOUSLY.**

This, then, is the biblical story of evil. There exist personal evil beings in the form of Satan and other demons. These creatures are created angels who have rebelled against God and now seek to corrupt both God's people and God's material creation. Because human beings themselves have joined the rebellion against God, humans now have the capacity to bring forth evil as well. Therefore, evil now comes to us from three sources: demons, humanity, and the corrupted world. We experience demonic oppression, human sin, and natural disasters both big and small, making evil both personal and systemic, natural and supernatural, opposed to God and yet still subject to God.

PERCEIVING THE THREAT OF EVIL

People tend to make one of three mistakes when they start thinking about how to respond to the threat of evil in the world.[11]

> **Optimism:** We might say, *It's not that bad. It's a misunderstanding. If we had better education, better systems, more prosperity, more comfort, evil would go away.* This view embraces the narrative of **cultural progress**: with the right stuff in place, we can eradicate evil! Things are going to get better!

> **Cynicism:** We feel totally overwhelmed by all that is wrong with the world and give in to despair. This view embraces the narrative of **cultural decline**: no matter how hard we work, there's more bad stuff out there than good stuff. Things are going to get worse.

Narcissism: We see ourselves (and people like us) as the answer to evil. This view embraces the narrative of **tribalism**: if more people were like *me*, this world would be a better place.

People move through all three of these in various stages of their lives. We go through cycles where we optimistically think we can organize and work the evil out of the world. When that fails, we become cynical and despair. Despair eventually turns to bitterness and anger, which requires an object. So, we turn our fury on [insert scapegoat group here: liberals, conservatives, immigrants, poor people, rich people, white people, black people, Muslims, Latinos, etc.]. Our anger flows from the narcissistic belief that if other people "got it" the way we "get it," then there wouldn't be evil in the world.

What is tragic is that so many Christians have been swept up into this kind of thinking. Even Christians who don't play along with the culture wars of Western society still fall prey to this kind of self-righteous thinking. Christians often see the problem of evil and think that they and the *church* are the answer.

> THE CHURCH IS NOT THE ANSWER TO THE PROBLEM OF EVIL. THE GOSPEL IS THE ANSWER TO THE PROBLEM OF EVIL.

Fellow brothers and sisters in Christ, let us be absolutely clear. We are *not* the answer. The church is not the answer to the problem of evil. The *gospel* is the answer to the problem of evil, not the church. The church is the body of people who believe the gospel, are rescued by the gospel, seek to live the gospel, and share the gospel. But we ourselves are not the answer.

N. T. Wright puts it well:

> Jesus' way for his followers is that they, too, recognize
> evil for what it is, and that they learn to pray, Deliver
> Us from Evil. To omit the petitions about "testing" and
> "evil" off the end of the Lord's prayer would indicate
> the first wrong route; to make them the only significant
> part of the prayer would be the second wrong route; to
> see yourself as the answer to the prayer, as the people
> through whose virtue the world will be delivered from
> evil, would be the third.[12]

We must not face evil with optimism, cynicism, or narcissism.
We cannot fix this, all is not lost, and we are not the answer. If
that's the case, then what should we do?

TEMPTATION & EVIL

Consider the phrase "lead us not into temptation." That word
temptation in the original Greek is *peirasmos*. It means something akin to "enticement, trial, adversity, affliction, or trouble."[13]
Therefore, we might translate this line of the Lord's Prayer a bit
more literally as, "Save us from the great time of trial."[14]

The idea here is not the kind of general temptation to do
stupid, petty, wicked, and sinful things, but rather the ultimate
temptation: the great trial of life which is the truest and deepest
form of temptation in which we stare into the void of suffering
and death and know we cannot escape.

Therefore, "Lead us not into temptation" has been interpreted
as "rescue us from eternal death."

While some Christians may not be familiar with this interpretation, we can lean on the Reformers Martin Luther and John Calvin, and more recently Karl Barth and N. T. Wright, who can help close the gap in the average Protestant understanding of the Lord's Prayer. In Calvin's section on the Lord's Prayer in his *Institutes of the Christian Religion*, he writes:

> It is not in our power to engage that great warrior the devil in combat, or to bear his force or onslaught.... Now we seek to be freed from his power, as from the jaws of a mad and raging lion (1 Peter 5:8); if the Lord did not snatch us from the midst of death, we could not help being immediately torn to pieces by his fangs and claws, and swallowed down his throat.[15]

In the same way, the second phrase "but deliver us from evil" is worth closely examining. Evil in this sense does not mean small evils. Petty selfishness is not the same thing as evil or the evil one. First Peter 5:8 reads: "Your adversary the devil prowls around like a roaring lion, seeking someone to devour." The image is of Satan prowling like a ravenous beast. He is the evil one who is stronger than you. The original Greek word *rhuomai* means not only "deliver us," but more viscerally, "snatch us from these jaws."[16] Put it all together and you get an expanded translation that is something to this effect: "Save us from the ultimate trial, which is too much for us to bear; snatch us from the jaws of the evil one who would devour us."

Karl Barth puts powerfully poetic language to this idea:

> Spare us not from struggle (which we must accept),
> not from sufferings (which we must endure), but

spare us from the encounter with this enemy, who is stronger than all our strength, more clever than all our intelligence, more dangerously sentimental than we ourselves are capable of being. He is more pious than all our Christian piety, both ancient and modern, or theological. Shield us from all possibility of evil from which we know not how to preserve ourselves, since it would utterly and irrevocably degrade us.[17]

There is an ultimate trial that all of us will fail, and there is an ultimate enemy who is far too dangerous for us to handle. No amount of discipline, biblical study, prayer, virtue, good deeds, social justice, generosity, or self-control will save you. Life will end in death, and there is a monster who is waiting to consume you. This is the true threat of evil. It is far deeper and more powerful and yet far subtler and more devious than anything else you and I will encounter in life. We think we live in a world with lots of medium-sized evils and medium-sized enemies. But the story of the Bible, which is the story of our world, tells a far more frightening tale: there is a singular deep evil (sin that leads to death) and a singular strong enemy (the devil and his demons).

So we've at least come a bit closer to understanding the story of evil, and now we've perceived the threat of evil. It's time to ask the question: What is God going to do about all of this? If God is still sovereign, which is to say "If God is still God," what is *His* response to evil? What we'll see is that, even in a world corrupted by evil, inhabited by people who commit evils, and plagued by the prince of evil, God can still bring redemption.

HOPE FOR REDEMPTION FROM EVIL

God takes on human flesh and enters His world, not as a crusader come to fight evil, but as a vulnerable human baby. Jesus was born into evil times. King Herod tried to kill Him, and His family fled as refugees of infanticide to Egypt. He grew up in rural poverty. Nazareth was a backwater, insignificant little township. Jesus was raised the son of a carpenter. He was a blue collar, working class, brown-skinned man who made His living doing manual labor. Christ lived under Roman occupation. Jesus' experience of evil did not begin with His ministry; it began with His birth. He was a hunted, impoverished, and oppressed racial and religious minority. But then, at the right time, He responded to the call of God the Father and "led up by the Spirit into the wilderness to be tempted by the devil."[18] He was taking up, in Himself, the vocation of God's people to be faithful in the time of trial, or *peirasmos*. We pray that God would not lead us into this temptation, but the Spirit of God led Jesus there. Jesus' ministry begins with His entering the *peirasmos*.

Times of trial serve as bookends to the earthly ministry of Jesus. Before Jesus enters the garden of Gethsemane to pray, He tells His disciples, "Watch and pray that you may not enter into temptation."[19] The Roman Catholic theologian Hans Urs von Balthasar puts it this way: "Jesus prays in the peirasmos, whereas the disciples pray to be preserved from it."[20]

In the infanticide surrounding His birth, in the temptation of the wilderness, in agony of the garden of Gethsemane, and in the suffering of the cross, Jesus faced great evil. He faced the great time of trial. He faced the prowling beast who seeks to consume every good, true, and beautiful thing that God has made.

Jesus faced the beast; He stared into the jaws of death and . . . what?

He allowed Himself to be swallowed.

He allowed Himself to be rent and torn and crushed to death.

Jesus instructed His followers to pray, "Lead us not into temptation, but deliver us from evil." In the garden of Gethsemane, He prayed a version of this stanza when He asked God the Father to spare Him from what lay ahead at the cross. God's answer to Jesus' prayer was "no," so that His answer to your prayer would be "yes." Jesus was led into the trial to face evil so that we would be spared.

Friends, this is how the gospel subverts evil. Jesus did not come to fight evil with a sword, and even His disciples had a hard time wrapping their imaginations around that one. We all tend to think with the same logic as Peter: if there is evil, we must defeat it.

This is not the imagination of Jesus. Jesus instead shows that where there is evil, it may be subverted by loving sacrifice. Jesus doesn't fight death, He goes into the belly of death, and in His resurrection, He blows it up from the inside. This is the good news of the subversive gospel, and this is why the church must be the people who:

> Receive the gospel with gratitude, marveling that there is a God who loves us so much as to allow Himself to be devoured by death so that we might live.

> Embody the gospel in our habits and practices and lifestyles and calendars and vocations, always seeking to live out this kind of subversive love in the midst of the evils of our world.

Extend the gospel, offering the gospel of Jesus as the answer to evil and not ourselves, our church, or goodness knows, not our politics!

We must offer Christ Himself as the answer to evil.

SUBVERSIVELY RESISTING EVIL IN ALL FORMS

Time for a little subversive reimagining. In 1 Peter 5:9–10, we read:

Resist him, firm in your faith, knowing that the same kinds of suffering are being experienced by your brotherhood throughout the world. And after you have suffered a little while, the God of all grace, who has called you to his eternal glory in Christ, will himself restore, confirm, strengthen, and establish you.

The church must resist evil. How? Firmly in our faith. What faith? Faith in the gospel and faith in the God who suffered for us, who did what we cannot do. Faith in the God who was led into temptation and who was *not* delivered from evil. Faith in the God who now listens to us when we pray and who says yes and who has the power to deliver us when we cry out to Him.

Therefore, we can resist personal evil from the devil and demons. We can pray against demonic oppression, and even though we know self-consciously that our neighbors may think we're insane, we can pray for their protection and freedom.

We resist personal evil from other

WE REFUSE TO BELIEVE THE SECULAR VERSION OF REALITY THAT SLAPS A CEILING AND FLOOR ON THE WORLD AND SAYS THERE IS NOTHING ABOVE OR BELOW AND INSISTS THAT SPIRITUALITY CAN BE EXPLAINED AWAY BY HUMAN PSYCHOLOGY.

people. Not with a sword, but with love of enemies. Not fighting evil with evil, but overcoming evil with good.

We resist systemic evil in all its forms. We study history, we study culture, and we take institutions, economics, politics, and education seriously. We work to root out systemic evil wherever we find it.

We resist natural evil. We pray against tsunamis, viruses, cancers, floods, and earthquakes. We pray for the Lord to show mercy and power. We pray for healing for all who are sick and courage for all who are dying.

We resist supernatural evil. We refuse to believe the secular version of reality that slaps a ceiling and floor on the world and says there is nothing above or below and insists that spirituality can be explained away by human psychology. Instead, we pray against the evil principalities and powers of this world: *may they be overthrown and may God's kingdom come.*

We resist all evils that oppose God, and we do so while knowing that our God is sovereign over evil, that He has overcome the ultimate temptation and evil and so is able to redeem evil for His good purposes.

FACING EVIL WITH HUMILITY & CONFIDENCE

This means, in the power of the gospel of Jesus' love for us, the church is able to resist evil, even the very great evils of our time, with humble confidence. The church can and should be humble, knowing we are weak and our enemy is strong. We must be humble, knowing that it is only by the death and resurrection of Jesus that we are snatched from the jaws of eternal death.

But buried within that humility is an unshakable confidence.

The church can and should be confident, because our God is sovereign, and Christ is the King. He has promised that, in all things, He is working for the good of those who love Him and who have been called according to His purposes. In fact, the church *must* be confident because the death and resurrection of Christ anticipate the future final downfall of evil. The resurrection of Jesus is just the first of many resurrections that are to come, when all who belong to Jesus will rise and earth itself will be made new—a place of goodness and beauty, no longer stained by evil.

In that great and glorious day, there will be:

- No more personal evil—the devil and his demons finally defeated.
- No more human evil—weapons of war turned into gardening tools.
- No more systemic evil—all instruments of oppression, racism, sexism, poverty . . . vanished.
- No more natural evil—no more floods, earthquakes, no more viruses.
- No more supernatural oppression—nothing to fear at all.
- Fear itself dissolved into security, trust, and peace.
- There will be none who oppose God, and therefore, there will be none who oppose what is good.

We live in evil times, as all the people of God have always lived in evil times. There are many fearful things surrounding us and within us. We have many small enemies and one, true, real enemy. But we need not live in fear. You do not have to be an anxious person no matter how much evil threatens to harm you because: God loves you, He has given Himself for you, and if your faith is in the gospel of Jesus, then when you pray, "Lead us not into temptation, but deliver us from evil." God's answer is yes.

Alleluia. Amen.

QUESTIONS FOR DISCUSSION

1. What forms of evil are you prone to dismiss? How does this make you more likely to both participate in these forms of evil and to be harmed by them?

2. Where are you in the three-part cycle of optimism, cynicism, and narcissism in response to evil in the world?

3. How is Jesus' subversive approach to evil different from what most Christians tend to do?

4. How would you describe the difference between your old imagination of deliverance from evil and the new imagination offered by this stanza of the Lord's Prayer?

PRAYER FOR MEDITATION HEAVENLY FATHER, we Your people are beset by many trials, temptations, and fears. We confess our hearts are anxious, timid, and easily swayed by the allure of false securities. By the power of the resurrection of Jesus from the dead, help us to resist the evils of the devil and the corruption of this world in all its forms. By the work of Your Spirit within us, instill in our hearts resilient courage to walk through the wilderness of this life with fearless, quiet confidence. All for the sake of Your love. Amen.

CHAPTER 9

REIMAGINING THE CHURCH AS POWERLESS

In a very real sense not one of us is qualified, but it seems that God continually chooses the most unqualified to do his work, to bear his glory. If we are qualified, we tend to think that we have done the job ourselves. If we are forced to accept our evident lack of qualification, then there's no danger that we will confuse God's work with our own, or God's glory with our own.

–MADELINE L'ENGLE

Our Father, who art in heaven,
hallowed be thy Name,
thy kingdom come,
thy will be done,
on earth as it is in heaven.
Give us this day our daily bread.
And forgive us our trespasses,
as we forgive those
who trespass against us.
And lead us not into temptation,
but deliver us from evil.
For thine is **THE KINGDOM, AND THE POWER, AND THE GLORY**,
for ever and ever. Amen.

From the safety of his bedroom window, the boy watched as the priest was led into the square and executed by firing squad. With all the parishes closed and the last priest killed, the church was officially dead. Heartbroken, he lay back on his bed and stared at the ceiling thinking of how there are no more priests, no more heroes, no more churches—they were all dead.

At this point, you, the reader, are a page and a half from the end of *The Power & the Glory* by Graham Green, which is a fictional story about a real time in history: the persecution of the Catholic church in the Tabasco region of Mexico in the 1930s. It is a book that feels like a slow and steady descent into darkness. And you can't help but think, as the reader: *I guess this is how it all ends.*

I think many followers of Jesus today live with this kind of deep existential dread when they think about the future of the church in our secular age. I have had more conversations than I can count with parishioners who, because of their faith, feel they are part of a rapidly shrinking, increasingly powerless, minority fringe group. I have heard very talented professionals say, "I don't know how much longer I can last in my field. As soon as my coworkers find out that I'm a Christian, I'm done." I've heard concerned parents say, "I don't know how to prepare my son or daughter for the kind of future they're going to have to navigate." I've heard more than one retired pastor say a version of, "I'm so glad I don't have to lead at a time like this. I'm glad I got out when I did." It seems that many followers of Jesus today, when it comes to their feelings about the future of the church, do not feel there is much to look forward to. When they look ahead, all they see are storm clouds. Martin Buber, on the eve of WWII, wrote: "We Jews know more deeply, more truly, that world history has not been turned upside down to its very foundations—that the world is not yet redeemed. We sense its unredeemedness."[1]

Yes, we could all say with Buber, we sense the world's unredeemedness.

What's more, as the church in the West is increasingly marginalized, we feel the loss of power and the loss of glory. Western Christians have largely grown accustomed to wielding political and cultural power; but now we find ourselves increasingly powerless. We feel that we are becoming small and despised. Faithful Christians are estranged from *both* major political parties and we're a complete oddity to mainstream culture. So many folks think and talk and write about how the glory of the American church is greatly diminished.

But it is exactly that kind of thinking that is undermined by the gospel in the Lord's Prayer—especially in the final stanza. This final doxology sums up the entirety of the Lord's Prayer and shows us how the gospel subverts our worldly definition of how kingdoms are built, power is used, and glory is achieved.

The doxology traditionally goes like this: *For thine is the kingdom, and the power, and the glory, for ever and ever. Amen.* While not a direct quote from either version of the Lord's Prayer in Matthew or Luke, the phrase is deeply biblical, and the source is theological and liturgical. It is theological in that, rather than draw on one verse, the phrase draws from the entire counsel of Scripture, which absolutely teaches that the kingdom, power, and glory belong to the Lord forever. It is liturgical because this phrase was added to the prayer in the context of corporate worship in local churches sometime during the first few centuries. The priest leading the worship service would say the portions of the prayer that are based on Scripture, and the congregation would respond with the closing doxology:

> The doxology constitutes an adjunction, an enlargement, introduced for the liturgical usage of the Lord's

Prayer. The congregation as a whole pronounced (or chanted) these words as a reply to the six petitions which were said by the celebrant.[2]

These grand words were added as a fitting theological summary to the Lord's Prayer by people who, themselves, did not possess any cultural or political power. The final doxology of the Lord's Prayer is truly a liturgy in the wilderness. It is the surprising praise of people who somehow were enjoying the glory of the risen Christ even though they themselves were not crowned with any kind of worldly glory. Why would a powerless people conclude the central prayer in the worship service with words of power and glory? If the early church (a persecuted minority fringe group if there ever was one) was to tack anything on the end of the Lord's Prayer, why didn't they add a phrase like: "And please let the next Caesar be a Christian!" or "Let us receive tax-exempt status!" or, on a less political note, *"Lord, let our witness to our neighbors be so powerful that they grow to respect us, love us, join us, and stop killing us. Amen."*

WE ALL CRAVE GLORY

Phil Jackson, former NBA coach of the Chicago Bulls and the Los Angeles Lakers, once said, "Sometimes winning is just as hard as losing, there isn't enough glory to go around."[3] Every human being comes with built-in hunger for glory. From the child on the trampoline yelling "Watch me, Daddy!" to the CEO boarding the corporate jet, to the scientists competing for the Nobel Prize … *every* human being craves glory.

And with good reason. Part of what it means for human

beings to bear the very image of God is to reflect an aspect of His glory. Humanity was given the authority to name creation and to rule over and steward creation. God Himself calls humanity good. From the lips of the Father we hear the affirmation that there is a unique glory to humanity that is different from, say, the glory of the Grand Tetons in Wyoming or the glory of an osprey in flight over the Chesapeake Bay. This glory undergirds our contemporary conception of human rights. Few people today realize that underneath many of the basic assumptions of Western society lies profoundly biblical theology. Talking about "human rights" is secular language for a much deeper biblical concept, which is the glory of humanity. Secularists say that people should not be oppressed because they have rights. Christians say people should not be oppressed because every human being is imbued with God-given glory.

But even though we were made glorious, we wanted more glory. In Genesis 3, we see the first temptation: eat this, gain knowledge, be like God (translation: wouldn't you like to have more glory? Here's a shortcut to glory, eat this it will make you more powerful and with more power you will get more glory). And reach out we did, in an attempt to gain more power and glory for ourselves. After the fall into sin, the power-and-glory chase continues. Cain wields power over Abel because he is jealous of Abel's glory. The whole human race puts forth a coordinated effort with the tower of Babel (i.e., *let's use our power to make a name for ourselves*). In the book of Exodus, we meet Pharaoh, drunk with power and glory but fearful he will lose it. In the prophetic book of Daniel, we meet Nebuchadnezzar who builds a golden image of himself and threatens to incinerate anyone who refused to worship it. Talk about a power and glory trip! When we reach the New Testament, consider how the gospel of Luke begins: "In those days, a decree went out from Caesar Augustus that all the world should be registered."[4] Who is Caesar Augustus? He was the one who did what nobody had done for two hundred years: he united the Roman Empire in peace. The Roman Empire was a greater kingdom than the tower of Babel. Caesar had more power than Pharaoh in Egypt. He had more worldly glory than Nebuchadnezzar in Babylon. Caesar is a fulfillment of humanity's pursuit of glory through power. No wonder Caesar held the title "The Son of God." And how did he get there? He used power to gain glory. He killed his enemies, he manipulated his friends, and he leveraged all his resources.

NOT MUCH HAS CHANGED

Has anything really changed? Consider the average politician today. Are they not often people who have already accumulated great wealth and power; and in launching a political career, are they not leveraging it to achieve even more power and, more importantly, glory? There are exceptions, but they prove the rule. Consider the latest wave of virtue-signaling businesses. Today, the companies that are highly respected are not only those that make money, but those that make money by doing something that will be praised. CEOs don't just want to be rich anymore, they also want to be *loved*. Which is to say, leaders don't just want power, they want glory. Isn't that interesting?

On a smaller scale: Consider the average neighborhood squabble between people who share an apartment wall or back alley. What is the disagreement? Is it not about power? Who gets to decide what should happen? Consider the power and glory dynamics at play within the two social media platforms of Facebook and Instagram. Facebook is about networking to increase your relational social power. Instagram is about glory, inviting people to give you glory for the beauty of who you are and wonder of what you do. If you've ever lived with a roommate or a spouse, do you know the peculiar delight when you catch them doing something you've both agreed not to do? Why is that so delicious? Because now you have a leg up! You have a measure of power over them.

If you have ever parented or cared for young children, then you might also know the all-too-common experience of using your power as an adult to overwhelm a child and win a disagreement. From Caesar to your next-door neighbor to you; from the corporate boardroom, to social media, to the kitchen table—all of us are still chasing power and glory.

GIVING UP POWER TO SHARE GLORY

Why do we do these things? Why are we never satisfied with whatever measure of power and glory life has granted us? The apostle Paul gives us the hard truth in Romans 1:21: "For although they knew God, they did not honor him as God or give thanks to him, but they became futile in their thinking, and their foolish hearts were darkened." Instead of using our God-given power to give glory to God (our creational design), we have used our power to glorify ourselves (a distortion of our design). In the midst of that distortion, Jesus comes to us, and through His church, invites us to pray about power and glory in the closing stanza of the Lord's Prayer. How can you and I genuinely and authentically pray words like these?

The answer is found in a surprising inversion: while we use power to gain glory, God gives up power to share glory.

Let's look at the narrative arc of the gospel of Luke. What happens at the incarnation? The Son "emptied himself, by taking the form of a servant, being born in the likeness of men."[5] Christ entered this world as a vulnerable, powerless child to lower-middle class parents of an oppressed religious and cultural minority. Luke's gospel is the story of parallel kings, parallel kingdoms, two different uses of power, and two different kinds of glory. This account begins with Caesar and with his power and glory in the Roman Empire. Then the author brings in Jesus as the foil, the rising contender. So, when the angels proclaim, "Glory to God in the highest!" we, the listeners, are meant to hear this exclamation of praise *in opposition to* the power and glory of Caesar.

Consider how the ministry of Jesus begins. In Luke 4, Jesus is tempted by Satan to wield power to achieve glory. He declines.

Consider who Jesus calls as His disciples. Are they the smartest, the best, and the most well networked? No, they are the lower working class and the social outcasts.

Jesus goes to great lengths to keep His power a secret. When He casts out demons, He silences them so that no one will know He is the Christ. When He heals a leper, He commands the restored man to tell no one. Why? Because He is using His power to set others free, not to gain glory.

In Luke 9:48, the disciples are arguing about which one is the greatest. Jesus listens to their bickering, and in response, He picks up a child, sets the kid on His lap, and says, "For he who is least among you all is the one who is great." In Luke 22, the disciples argue about who is the greatest *again*. This time, Jesus says, "The kings of the Gentiles exercise lordship over them, and those in authority over them are called benefactors. But not so with you. Rather, let the greatest among you become as the youngest, and the leader as the one who serves."[6] Jesus wants to drive the point home, telling them, *Power and glory work differently in My kingdom.*

Think about Jesus' encounters with power after He was arrested:

- When He was brought before the council of Pharisees and Sadducees, He was facing the spiritual power of the people.
- When He appeared before King Herod, He was facing the cultural power of society.
- When He was taken before Pontius Pilate, He was facing the political power of the empire.

Isn't it interesting that, in Luke 23:12, Herod and Pilate became friends the day they both encountered Jesus? Like bullies bonding over kicking in a nerd's teeth, what brought them together was the power they wielded over Jesus. The trial of Christ is a confrontation of powers. Reading the entire gospel of Luke is like watching one long, slow collision course of worldly power versus the power of God. It feels like watching a freight train collide with an apple in slow motion. Caesar and Rome are the freight train; Jesus is the apple.

Crucifixion was a symbol of Roman power and a kind of sick glory. Crucifixion says, "Rome can do anything it wants to you."

The glory of Rome was that its power was ultimate. It could strip your dignity and end your life. On the cross, Jesus, God in the flesh, surrendered His power, and His glory was extinguished. The cross appears to conclusively prove that the kingdom, the power, and the glory are decidedly *not* God's.

However, there is Easter. God the Father raises Jesus the Son from the dead. Before Christ ascends into heaven, He tells His disciples, "I am sending the promise of my Father upon you. But stay in the city until you are clothed with power from on high."[7] In His resurrection, Jesus is powerful and glorious. But what does He do with His resurrection power and glory? He immediately promises to share it!

Our Lord makes good on His promise in sending the power of His Holy Spirit at Pentecost. The indwelling of the Spirit of the risen Christ in the church today is testament to the heart of God that desires, not to hoard, but to share His power.

Additionally, Christ has promised to glorify His church upon His return. The future of the church is wondrously glorious!

> "Come, I will show you the Bride, the wife of the Lamb."
> And he carried me away in the Spirit to a great, high
> mountain, and showed me the holy city Jerusalem
> coming down out of heaven from God, having the glory
> of God.[8]

The Bride, the wife of the Lamb, the Holy City, the new Jerusalem . . . these are consummated images of the church, the redeemed of Jesus. This beautiful community is radiating with the glory of God. Beaten and downtrodden no longer, this is a vision of the church triumphant.

SUBVERSIVE POWER & GLORY

So you see, the way of our world is to use power to gain glory, but the way of Jesus is to give up power in order to share glory. This is the subversive gospel. The gospel does not combat the powers of the world head-on, it rather subverts power by giving it away. The gospel does not vie with the glory of this world in bizarre beauty contest (i.e., who's living a happier, fulfilled life: Christians or non-Christians?). No. Rather, the gospel holds up a weak, broken person in a backwater neighborhood who prays and works faithfully at an undesirable job to take care of too many children, and aging parents, and annoying neighbors . . . and says to the glamorous world of success and carefully managed images, *this* is what glory looks like.

In the kingdom of God, the first shall be last, the strong must become weak, the rich must become poor, and the full must become empty. The cross and the resurrection of Jesus turn power and glory on their head.

REIMAGINING THE WORLD
THROUGH GOSPEL POWER & GLORY

With the closing line of the Lord's Prayer, the stakes cannot get any higher for any who dare to pray it. Personal kingdom-building, power, and glory are what we all want. Therefore, it's no small thing to conclude our prayer with a surrender, that these be given, not to us, but to God. This is the final stamp on the envelope, the nail in the coffin, the authorities have surrounded the escaped convict, and the game is up. This prayer has chased me down, line after line, while my soul has ducked and dodged in a desperate attempt to avoid being caught by the sheer compre-hensiveness of this prayer; given by the God and prayed to the God who refuses to get on board with my agenda, but lovingly, and persistently, invites me into His. The closing doxology confronts me; it asks me if I have truly surrendered in full. This is the final check before launch.

The prayer is nearly finished. Soon the pray-er will rise from their knees and return to work. Are they going to say "Amen" and immediately return to their own kingdom, power, and glory? Will they be conscripted into participating in the kingdom, power, and glory of our secular age? Or have they been so shaped by this prayer that they, perhaps, ready to do a little subversive reimagining of their own? As N. T. Wright appropriately points out, "If the church isn't prepared to subvert the kingdoms of the world with the kingdom of God, the only honest thing would be to give up praying this prayer altogether, especially its final doxology."[9] What does it look like for the church to subversively embody the final stanza of the prayer? We must begin to imagine an invisible kingdom, a powerless people, and an unglorified church.

> **PERSONAL KINGDOM-BUILDING, POWER, AND GLORY ARE WHAT WE ALL WANT. IT'S NO SMALL THING TO CONCLUDE OUR PRAYER WITH A SURRENDER, THAT THESE BE GIVEN, NOT TO US, BUT TO GOD.**

An Invisible Kingdom: We are not seeking to build a visible, Christian empire in our cities, or in the United States of America, or anywhere on planet earth. We are seeking the kingdom of God, which we cannot see, but in which we nonetheless participate.

A Powerless People: The Christian life begins with a surrender of power. In baptism, we surrender our power of autonomy (we need God to save us), self-determinism (we are no longer in charge of our lives), and individualism (we are baptized into the family of God); and it is sustained by Holy Communion, where we come empty-handed to receive the fruits of God surrendering His own power in the broken body and poured out blood of Jesus. Author Andy Crouch says it well: "The sacraments of the church are rehearsals of the end of power, putting our own power to death in our baptism and then approaching with trembling awe the memorial of the moment when God's own Son gave up his power."[10] If this is true, then how then could we go about the rest of our lives seeking power at work, in politics, in culture, at home, in our marriages, in our families, and in our neighborhoods? The church is, by definition, a powerless people.

An Inglorious Church: The church is also, while we remain in this world, deliberately unglorified. We might say that we are a glory-less church. If we are a body of people who have surrendered our power (and therefore have no means of achieving glory), who are following a Lord who did not use power to glorify Himself (but rather received glory from the power of the Father), and who in turn shares that glory with us ... then how could we go out seeking any form of worldly glory for ourselves? How could we possibly go out and believe that the church is due some respect or admiration from the world?

Dear friends, the church does not seek her own glory! We must settle in for the long road of participating in a belittled church, a seemingly ineffectual church, a church that isn't respected, admired, appreciated, loved by our cities, country, or world. An inglorious church.

GIVE IT AWAY

We must be a church that receives no glory because we are too preoccupied with *giving it away*. This happens when we adopt postures of quiet simplicity and humility. You cannot strive for these virtues; you must sink down into them—embracing your smallness.

> The highest glory of the creature is in being only a vessel, to receive and enjoy and show forth the glory of God. It can do this only as it is willing to be nothing in itself, that God may be all. Water always fills the lowest places. The lower, the emptier a man lies before God, the speedier and fuller will be the inflow of divine glory.[11]

When we sink down into the posture of quiet, simple, humble smallness, we experience a kind of strange glory that our secular age finds incomprehensible. It is like the glory of an elderly woman's face creased by eighty years of smiling. It is like the glory of a young man who returns home exhausted by the day's work, and then washes the dirty dishes. It is the like glory of a child who loses her soccer game and, fighting back tears, tells the other team they played well. It is like the glory of the nurse who stays an extra hour after a twelve-hour shift to listen to a patient who wanted someone to talk to. Our secular age will brush these off as trite sentimentality and then give its attention to the latest celebrity. But the glory of the Creator will flow in and through His beloved creatures who make much of Him and much of others and little of themselves.

And when these little people gather together as the church, they give glory to God in worship: singing, praying, playing musical instruments, shouting, laughing, weeping, eating, drinking, feasting because they are *enjoying* the glory and beauty and wonder of their God. The church truly gives glory to God when it gives little thought to itself and no thought at all to its own glory.

The church also gives glory to neighbors. A church sees in every human being the glory of the image of God. The church recognizes that glory in the other. The church names that glory, draws out that glory, and celebrates that glory! The church shares, gives, and enjoys the glory of neighbors, especially the neighbors whom the world has deemed inglorious. The church shares the glory of God with those whom the world judges unworthy of glory.

DARKNESS BEFORE THE DAWN

In one of the final scenes of Graham Green's *The Power & the Glory*, there is a surprising knock at the door. (Remember, the young boy has just witnessed the last remaining priest executed and believes that the church is dead.) The boy gets out of bed and opens the door. Standing in the entrance is a new priest . . . and just like that, the book ends.

The arrival of the new priest at the conclusion of the book leaves the reader with the powerful image of how the church will go on and on—the gates of hell will not prevail against it. God's power and glory will win out.

If we believe the subversive gospel—if we are seeking an invisible kingdom, as a powerless people, in the inglorious church—then we will, no doubt, feel like we are *losing* most of the time. We will feel like things are getting worse and worse. When this happens, we must not lose heart! We must remember that, for the disciples, the most discouraging, powerless, glory-less moment came when Jesus was on the cross, poised on the precipice of overcoming the power of death and triumphing in glory. It felt like losing, but victory was at hand. It is always darkest before the dawn.

QUESTIONS FOR DISCUSSION

1. Where do you most sense the world's "unredeemedness"?
2. Where do you wish you had more power to make things go your way?
3. Where do you crave the glory of recognition, admiration, respect, and love?
4. How does the idea of being powerless make you feel?
5. What is one way you can give glory to a neighbor or coworker that other people would deem unworthy of glory?

PRAYER FOR MEDITATION ALMIGHTY GOD, we confess our hunger for power and our resentment toward those who wield power over us. Help us, by the willing sacrifice of Jesus, to relinquish our own pursuits of power and give ourselves in humble submission to You and to each other. Grant, by Your Spirit, that we may be content merely to reflect Your great glory to this world, that You may receive the honor due to Your name. Amen.

WALKING BACKWARD INTO THE FUTURE

Ka mua, ka muri
(Walking backward into the future)
-MAORI PROVERB

The Maori people of New Zealand use the above phrase to describe the posture of a wise person as he or she moves through life. There is a more difficult to pronounce phrase that spells out the concept a bit more explicitly: *Kia whakatomuri te haere ki mua* (To walk into the future our eyes must be fixed on the past). All of us, despite our various theological, denominational, political, cultural, racial, and economic locations, would sincerely like to be well prepared for whatever future is rushing to meet us. Agreed?

If the Maoris are right (and they are), then the resources for this do not lie in front of us, but behind us. Followers of Jesus today do not need to innovate their way into the future. We do not need to perpetually invent new, strange, desperate contortions of the Christian faith in order to adapt to our current cultural moment. The secular age in which we dwell need not be the shaper of our imaginations. We may do the number one thing that God calls His people to do over and over again throughout the Old Testament: *remember*. Which is to say, we may walk backward into the future with our eyes fixed, not on the dark, threatening clouds ahead, but on the weathered storms of the past.

In looking back, we will find better resources for our imaginations. None of us can predict the future; so, facing forward can only fill our imaginations with (at best) curiosity and (at worst) anxiety and fear. Looking back does not mean we want to re-create the past, nor does it mean we want to slow time down and avoid the future. No! We must move forward with real courage and determination.

The best possible way for us to move forward into the unknown is to allow our imaginations to be shaped by the most significant past—the surprising and subversive wonder of the gospel of Jesus. And the most powerful tool for shaping imaginations with the gospel has always been prayer. And the most potent, foundational prayer for any follower of Jesus is the Lord's Prayer. To be clear, prayer is not the only tool for shaping imaginations—art, music, literature, community, food, the natural world, and work all have their place. And, of course, the Lord's Prayer is certainly not the only way to pray; there are other liturgies, and extemporaneous, improvised prayers will always have a place in the life of a follower of Jesus. But the Lord's Prayer is the starting place: for prayer, for shaping the imagination, for navigating the present . . . and for preparing for the future.

When we pray the Lord's Prayer, we are planting seeds that can split concrete. We are dripping water that can wear away granite. We are shifting spiritual tectonic plates that lie deep underneath culture, society, and the depths of our own hearts. When we pray the Lord's Prayer, our imaginations are stirred, moved, and transformed. We begin to *see* the world differently; the way Jesus saw it. This means we can begin to engage our world the way Jesus did. I suppose that's another way of saying we can live out the gospel.

THE MOST POWERFUL TOOL FOR SHAPING IMAGINATIONS WITH THE GOSPEL HAS ALWAYS BEEN PRAYER. AND THE MOST POTENT, FOUNDATIONAL PRAYER IS THE LORD'S PRAYER.

When we pray the Lord's Prayer and then begin to live it out, we subvert the empire of this world, the City of Man, the kingdom of darkness. We do it, not by force, or by conquest, but by loving sacrifice—because that is the subversive way of our Lord.

ACKNOWLEDGMENTS

Thank you, Don Gates and Amy Simpson, for your initial encouragement and advice. There would be no book without you.

Thank you, Trillia Newbell and Amanda Cleary Eastep, for patiently enduring my endless questions and for generously lending your intelligence and skill to this project. Thank you to the whole team at Moody—what a privilege to work with you!

To the good people of Redeemer Anglican Church, to the Vestry, clergy, staff, and laity—what a privilege to be your pastor!

Thank you to friends who suggested much needed improvements and saved me from many errors: Ben Lansing, Danny Hindman, Lewis Lovett, Justin Early, Liz Gray, Jon Thompson, Matt Smethurst.

Thank you to my colleagues: John Yates III, Tommy Hinson, Sam Ferguson, David Glade, and Tim Soots. Preaching through the Lord's Prayer with you brothers during a COVID quarantine was a lifeline for me in a dark season.

Thank you to Mamie, my grandmother on my father's side, who read *The Hobbit* aloud to me and taught me to love books.

Thank you to Mr. Palmer, my sixth-grade English teacher, who impressed upon me the joy of words.

Thank you to my dear siblings and in-laws: Michael and Liz Marotta, Caitlin and David Loughin, Alyse and Dom Gianino, who read the rough draft, offered helpful suggestions, and have tolerated their older brother's ramblings for many long years.

Thank you, Mom, for teaching me how to read the Bible and to pray. Thank you, Dad, for showing me what it means to be disciplined and selfless, to keep working at something long after weariness has set in. I am blessed to have such wonderful parents.

Thank you to my beautiful, witty, generous Rachel. With every passing year, I grow more astonished at my good fortune in marrying you. God has been so good to me.

Thank you to my lovely and clever daughters, June and Selah Rose. You are my sunshine.

Thank you to my brave and wise sons, Wills and John. You are my pride and joy.

And it seems right to add a thank you to Rivers, the family dog, who at the slow, gray age of twelve years, laid at my feet for most of the writing of this book. You are indeed a good boy. Rest in peace, buddy.

Praise God from whom all blessings flow
Praise Him all creatures here below
Praise Him above ye heavenly hosts
Praise Father, Son, and Holy Ghost.
Amen.

NOTES

The Lord's Prayer

"The Lord's Prayer," *The Book of Common Prayer* (Huntington Beach, CA: Anglican Liturgy Press, 2019), 21.

Introduction

1. Alissa Fowers and William Wan, "A Third of Americans Now Show Signs of Clinical Anxiety or Depression," *Washington Post*, May 26, 2020, https://www.washingtonpost.com/health/2020/05/26/americans-with-depression-anxiety-pandemic.

2. C. S. Lewis, *The Silver Chair* (New York: HarperCollins, 2002), 151–59.

3. Aaron Earls, "Small, Struggling Congregations Fill U.S. Church Landscape," LifeWay Research, March 6, 2019, https://lifewayresearch.com/2019/03/06/small-struggling-congregations-fill-us-church-landscape.

4. Timothy Keller, *How to Reach the West Again* (New York: Redeemer City to City, 2020), 5.

5. Isaiah 41:10.

6. C. S. Lewis, *The Voyage of the Dawn Treader* (New York: HarperTrophy, 2000), 186.

7. From *Ante-Nicene Fathers*, vol. 7, eds. Alexander Roberts, James Donaldson, and A. Cleveland Coxe, trans. M. B. Riddle (Buffalo, NY: Christian Literature Publishing Co., 1886). Rev. and ed. for New Advent by Kevin Knight, http://www.newadvent.org/fathers/0714.htm.

8. There is no written evidence that Archilochus said this, but the saying has been passed down as folklore.

Chapter 1: The Need for Subversive Imagination

Epigraph: Michael Fryer, "The Subversive Power of Beauty," On Being, March 1, 2015, https://onbeing.org/blog/the-subversive-power-of-beauty.

1. From an interview with Guy Raz, "How I Built This," *NPR* podcast, May 11, 2020, https://www.npr.org/2020/04/22/841269281/impossible-foods-pat-brown.

2. I first learned of these three postures from Greg Thompson in his excellent, unpublished white paper, "The Church in Our Time," 2011.

3. Kano Jigoro, *Mind Over Muscle: Writings from the Founder of Judo*, ed. Naoki Murata (Tokyo: Kodansha, 2005), 39–40.

4. Fryer, "The Subversive Power of Beauty."

5. Isaiah 6:5.

6. Psalm 44:23.

7. Luke 14:15.

8. The formula is derived from a fifth-century monk, Prosper of Aquitaine. His original phrase was, *legem credenda lex statuat supplicandi*: "Let the rule of supplicating establish the rule of believing," Jacques Minge, Patrologia Latina, 51, col 209.

Chapter 2: Reimagining God as Shared

Epigraph 1: Wendell Berry, *The Wild Birds* (New York: North Point Press, 1989).

Epigraph 2: Address at his enthronement as Anglican archbishop of Cape Town (September 7, 1986).

1. Luke 11:1–2.

2. G. K. Chesterton, *What Is Wrong with the World?* (Manchester, NH: Sophia Institute Press, 2022), Part V.

3. John 1:12.

4. *To Be a Christian: An Anglican Catechism* (Wheaton, IL: Crossway, 2020), 69.

5. Arthur Marx, *Collier's*, "Groucho Is My Pop," October 13, 1951, Column 2, 14.

6. Isaiah 30:1.

Chapter 3: Reimagining God as Affectionate

Epigraph: *Remember the Titans*, directed by Boaz Yakin, produced by Jerry Bruckheimer, 2000.

1. Ronald F. Levant, "The New Psychology of Men," Professional Psychology: Research and Practice 27, 1996, 259–65.

2. Ibid.

3. J. B. Simmons, *The Awakening of Washington's Church* (J. B. Simmons, 2016), 2.

4. Matthew 4:8–10.

5. Matthew 22:19–21.

6. John 18:36.

7. "German Coast Guard Trainee—Sept. 5, 2006," YouTube video, https://www.youtube.com/watch?v=yR0lWICH3rY.

8. Psalm 103:13.

Chapter 4: Reimagining God as Beautiful

Epigraph: Fyodor Dostoevsky, *The Idiot* (New York: Bantam Classics, 1983), 370.

1. 2 Corinthians 6:16–18.

2. From the transcription of the 2005 Kenyon Commencement Address, written and delivered by David Foster Wallace, May 21, 2005, https://web.ics.purdue.edu/~drkelly/DFWKenyonAddress2005.pdf.

3. Parenthetical addition is aligned with the biblical author's intent to demonstrate that all (both men and women) are adopted by God.

4. Galatians 3:26.

5. 1 John 3:1–2.

6. "Prayer of Anselm of Canterbury," *The Book of Common Prayer* (Huntington Beach, CA: Anglican Liturgy Press, 2019), 642–83.

Chapter 5: Reimagining God as Good

Epigraph: Aldous Huxley, *The Perennial Philosophy* (New York: Harper Perennial Modern Classics, 2009), 289.

1. This quote is commonly attributed to Voltaire.

2. Matthew 11:3.

3. Matthew 11:11.

4. Matthew 11:5–6.

5. Lamin Sanneh, *Whose Religion Is Christianity?: The Gospel beyond the West* (Grand Rapids, MI: Eerdmans, 2003), 43.

6. Luke 17:20–21.

7. "Mr. James Duffy," *Proverbial* with Joshua Gibbs, podcast audio, April 13, 2020, https://podcasts.apple.com/us/podcast/mr-james-duffy/id1481266455?i=1000471343269.

8. Matthew 11:6.

9. C. S. Lewis, *The Great Divorce* (New York: HarperOne, 2001), 90.

10. Augustine, "Book XIV Chap. 28, Of the Nature of the Two Cities, The Earthly and the Heavenly," in *The City of God* (Edinburgh: T&T Clark, 1871), 47.

11. Mark Sayers, Episode 4, *This Cultural Moment* (podcast), February 27, 2018.

12. Flannery O'Connor, "My Dear God," *New Yorker*, September 16, 2013, https://www.newyorker.com/magazine/2013/09/16/my-dear-god.

Chapter 6: Reimagining the Wilderness as a Place of Bounty

Epigraph: Alexander Schmemann, *For the Life of the World* (Crestwood, NY: St. Vladamir's Seminary Press, 1963), 16.

1. N. T. Wright, *The Lord and His Prayer* (Grand Rapids, MI: Eerdmans, 1996), 36.

2. Martin Luther, *Luther's Small Catechism* (St. Louis, MO: Concordia, 2019), Fourth Petition.

3. Exodus 16:2.

4. Exodus 16:3.

5. A paraphrase of Genesis 3:12–13.

6. John 6:47–51.

7. Catechismus council, Trident., n. 4, ex St. Augustine, "De Catechizandis rudibus."

8. *Alone*, Season 2, Episode 1, The History Channel.

Chapter 7: Reimagining Life as Free

Epigraph: Henri Nouwen Society, August 30, 2021, https://henrinouwen.org/meditations/forgiveness.

1. "Mary Johnson and Oshea Israel," Storycorps (originally aired on May 20, 2011 on NPR's *Morning Edition*), https://storycorps.org/stories/mary-johnson-and-oshea-israel.

2. *Home Alone*, 1990, directed by Christopher Columbus, produced by John Hughes.

3. Claire Dederer, "What Do We Do with the Art of Monstrous Men?," *The Paris Review*, November 20, 2017, https://www.theparisreview.org/blog/2017/11/20/art-monstrous-men.

4. Ibid.

5. Bernard of Clairvaux, 12th century (Jesu dulcis memoria). Translated from Latin to German in Arndt's True Christianity. Translated from German to English by Anton W. Böhme (1712) and John Christian Jacobi (Psalmodia Germanica, 1720). The version derives from *A Collection of Psalms and Hymns Extracted from Various Authors*, by Martin Madan, 1760.

6. Michka Assayas, *Bono: In Conversation* (New York: Riverhead, 2005), ch. 11, https://gracetruth.blog/2014/01/26/bono-on-the-difference-between-grace-and-karma.

7. "Mary Johnson and Oshea Israel," Storycorps.

8. Ibid.

9. Robert Farrar Capon, *Between Noon and Three: Romance, Law, and the Outrage of Grace* (Grand Rapids, MI: Eerdmans, 1996), 7.

Chapter 8: Reimagining Ourselves as Safe

Epigraph: "Make the Devil Leave Me Alone," Traditional African American work song, www.secondhandsongs.com/work/237033.

1. James 1:13.

2. Romans 8:28.

3. Karl Barth, *Prayer* (Louisville, KY: Westminster John Knox Press, 2002), 60.

4. Andrew Delbanco, *The Death of Satan: How Americans Have Lost the Sense of Evil* (New York: Noonday, 1996), 3.

5. Mark 7:20–23.

6. Isaiah 59:8–9.

7. Esau McCaulley, "Why Christians Must Fight Systemic Racism," *New York Times*, July 18, 2021.

8. Luke 8:26–39; 9:37–43.

9. Proverbs 15:26.

10. 1 John 4:4.

11. I am grateful to the published scholarship of N. T. Wright in helping me see these categories.

12. N. T. Wright, *The Lord and His Prayer* (Grand Rapids, MI: Eerdmans, 1996), 71.

13. "Peirasmos," Bible Hub, https://biblehub.com/greek/3986.htm.

14. Translation mine.

15. John Calvin, *Institutes of the Christian Religion*, vol. 2, ed. John T. McNeill, translated and indexed by Ford Lewis Battles (Louisville, KY: Westminster John Knox Press, 2006), 914.

16. "Rhuomai," Bible Hub, https://biblehub.com/greek/4506.htm.

17. Barth, *Prayer*, 61–62.

18. Matthew 4:1.

19. Matthew 26:41.

20. Hans Urs von Balthasar, *Theo-drama: Theological Dramatic Theory* (San Francisco: Ignatius Press, 1990), 96.

Chapter 9: Reimagining the Church as Powerless

Epigraph: Madeline L'Engle, *Walking on Water: Reflections on Faith & Art* (Colorado Springs: Convergent Books, 2016), 62.

1. Jürgen Moltmann, *Israel's No: Jews and Jesus in an Unredeemed World* (New York: Harper & Row, 1990).

2. Karl Barth, *Prayer* (Louisville, KY: Westminster John Knox Press, 2002), 65.

3. Note: Although a source hasn't been located, the author recalls hearing Coach Jackson say this in an interview.

4. Luke 2:1.

5. Philippians 2:7.

6. Luke 22:25–26.

7. Luke 24:49.

8. Revelation 21:9–11.

9. N. T. Wright, *The Lord and His Prayer* (Grand Rapids, MI: Eerdmans, 2014), 67.

10. Andy Crouch, *Playing God: Redeeming the Gift of Power* (Downers Grove, IL: IVP, 2013), 272.

11. Andrew Murray, *Humility & Absolute Surrender* (Carol Stream, IL: Tyndale, 2005).

Epilogue: Walking Backward into the Future

Epigraph: Eleanor Jane Rainford, "Ka Mua, Ka Muri—Walking Backwards into the Future: An Environmental History of the South Wairarapa Region 1984–2016," Victoria University of Wellington, 2017, http://hdl.handle.net/10063/6929.

"The best association for the word sacramental is Jesus. Yes, Jesus—the wonderful grace of Jesus; the glory of Jesus, His face shining like the sun; the life of Jesus, overflowing like a thousand geysers into our world."

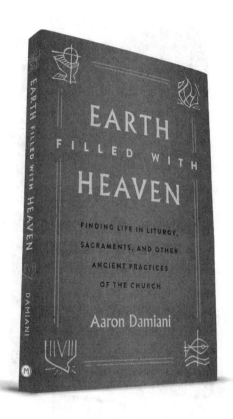

MOODY Publishers

From the Word to Life

Christians from a low-church background do not have to be afraid of liturgy and sacraments. On the contrary, these ancient ways of engaging with Scripture and faith help us see the beauty and taste the grace of heaven through the incarnation of Jesus. *Earth Filled with Heaven* is an evangelical introduction to the theological framework and habits of the sacramental life.

978-0-8024-2536-2 | also available as eBook and audiobook

HOW A CHANGING AND COMPLEX WORLD WILL CREATE A REMNANT OF RENEWED CHRISTIAN LEADERS

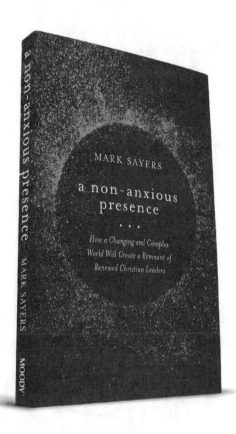

Crisis is a great revealer. It knocks us off our thrones. It uncovers weaknesses and brings to light idols. Yet amid the chaos of a crisis comes opportunity. Crisis always precedes renewal. See how that renewal happens—churches and leaders discover strategic ways to see our culture changed for Christ.

978-0-8024-2857-8 | also available as eBook and audiobook